WHERE'S MY FATHER?

Seeking and Finding God in the
Expected and Unexpected

written by
Gary Francis

WHERE'S MY FATHER?

Seeking and Finding God in the Expected and Unexpected

PENDIUM
PUBLISHING HOUSE
514-201 DANIELS STREET
RALEIGH, NC 27605

For information, please visit our Web site at
www.pendiumpublishing.com

PENDIUM Publishing and its logo
are registered trademarks.

Where's My Father?
by Gary Francis

ISBN: 978-1-944348-59-5

This book is printed on acid-free paper.

DEDICATION

To my students at Touching Miami with Love: I love you and I believe in you. I want you to know that God is with you. This book is a tangible expression of this reality: "You can do it, too!" I need you to understand this clearly. God has given you the opportunity to do great and inconceivable things. Seek after God. You will find him. He will do great things with your lives.

Devon and Izaiah, you've got this! It's now how you start the race, but it's how you finish it!

ACKNOWLEDGMENTS

As best I can, I want to express my deepest gratitude to the people who have made this book possible. There are many people to be thanked and the list really could be endless. However, I must limit myself to a few for now.

Isaac Edwards: Thank you, brother, for being the person who really prodded and inspired me to write this book. You believed in me and backed up your confidence in me with your words and actions. I am indebted to you for our conversations, writers' retreats, prayers, tears, and honest confessions we've shared as Jesus followers. All of these are interlaced into the words produced in this book. May this book serve as an answer to some of the prayers we have prayed.

Samuel Gray: Sam, I am in love with this book cover. You made my vision come alive. What you have produced is mesmerizing. Undoubtedly, this is art from my heart. Thank you for taking a heart expression and giving it life, vibrancy, and a message to be heard and seen through the eyes as well as the ears.

Rochelle Benjamin and David Carreño: Words can't express the appreciation I have for you two during the manuscript process. From start to finish, you were there. Your support, encouragement, and listening ears were just what I needed. Thank you, little cuzzo. *¡Gracias, hermano!*

Focus Group: Thank you, friends, for taking the time to read my manuscript and rough draft chapters. Your comments, suggestions, thoughts, phone calls, and emails were extremely helpful, skillful, and awe-inspiring. **Kristina Garrison, Joel Speizer, Auntie Jacqui, Terran Messer, Koen Goosens, and Michelle Girard**: Thank you for your help.

Mom (Joan Clarke) and **Trina Harris:** People won't always say it. However, I will. It definitely takes financial support to execute a project like this. Financial support and a whole lot of belief! This is my very first book venture and I am so grateful for your help in this endeavor.

Thank you, **Rose Marie Cole,** for connecting me to Pendium Publishing and the idea of releasing my book on Father's Day. Thank you, **Pendium Publishing**, for taking a chance with me, my words, and my story. You have made a dream into a reality.

And thank you, **Heavenly Father**, for your faithfulness to me. Thank you for the breath of life you have given me. Thank you for writing the pages of my life.

...You will seek me and find me, when you seek me with all your heart...

Jeremiah 29:13

CONTENTS

CHAPTER 1

Ian

Ian Francis. There are two clear memories that I have of actually seeing him. Both have to do with funerals. One funeral was for him. And the other was for a distant aunt on the maternal side of my family. Depressing, huh? Of the two memories, the clearest in my mind has to be my father's funeral. I remember it because it was so dramatic. It was like something out of a reality series or a weird movie. It was a heart-wrenching scene out of an award-winning feature film.

News came to me in the earlier part of November 2006 that my father was ill. He wasn't just sick. In fact, he could die from diabetes complications. His condition was so severe that he had lost some of his sight. And if memory serves me right, he actually went blind. Worse still, he had progressed to the point that he had to have both of his legs amputated.

The news I received about him did not alarm me at first. At least not in the forefront of my mind and heart. It bothered me somewhat, but not enough for me to change my schedule. When I look back on that time, I think I was a bit numb to what was really happening to him. During that time, I was studying for the Medical College Admission Test (MCAT) to get into medical school, so I was constructively and conveniently distracted.

It's hard to compute such an emotionally provoking concept when you are cramming your mind with endless tidbits of medical information. For me, it was a zero-to-sixty moment in my subconscious. All of a sudden, my father, who had not been present in my life, was spoken into existence. I didn't really know how to respond to it outwardly.

In my subconscious, the news was like God speaking the opening stanzas of existence— "Let there be light"— all over again. But instead of light, he was speaking, "Let Gary have a father" again. All of a sudden, consciousness of my biological father was a reality in my life again, but it was something that was absolutely foreign and absolutely weird. It was something that I couldn't prepare myself for, especially since his potentially imminent death was a large part of the preparation.

As stated, overall the news did not thwart my life direction and plans. However, the second and third reports definitely messed with me. In the second report, I was told my father had passed away. This promptly messed with my psyche. A lonely wind blew through that empty part of my life reserved for sonship. A life spent mostly without my father started to become the main topic in the forefront of my mind.

But a day later, I was perplexed. I was jolted, to say the least. I found out that the second report was possibly incorrect. What a shocker that was. I went from a brief moment of grief to an unexpected mountain of hope.

Knowing that he wasn't dead stirred something inside of me: the desire to see him; the desire to know him. The desire to be led by the man who birthed me was now on center stage of my life. All of a sudden, I felt an insatiable need to find a way to be close to him. Hanging in the atmosphere was a curious aspiration to reunite with him. This odd longing, by the way, was not a desire shared by some of the people I loved and who were closest to me. Or at the very least, they did not understand this desire well. From my perspective, my family did not respond the way I had hoped, especially my mother.

When I explained to my mom that I desperately wanted to see my father at his funeral she could not quite grasp why I would go to a funeral of someone who had never been in my life. I conceded that she had a point, an important one that made me realize something outstanding: absence *does* make the heart grow fonder. At least in my case.

In that window of time, the period of knowing that I could have my father back in my life, my heart was opened to a reality. I desperately wanted my father in my life, even if it were just for a brief moment. For better or worse, so much of what I desired in life was wrapped up in a person who was on a metaphorical permanent missing person report.

And then it got more complex. I got a final phone call, from my mother. *Brace yourself,* I thought. *Brace yourself...* because I wasn't ready for it. But maybe you will be. My mom did a very peculiar thing that day, a thing that killed me. A thing, to this day, I really have a hard time with. A thing that I was really confounded by.

Now before you get on to me too much, I love my mom. And I respect her a whole lot. But this was one of those moments that had me scratching my head. She called me to have a regular, run-of-the-mill conversation, the kind we have had a million times before. But this time there was a twist. In this conversation, we had the normal dialogue about life, the weather, how work was, and how the medical school process was going. And then she abruptly said, "by the way."

"...By the way, your father died." *By the way.* That's not a "by the way" type of thing. But she said it just that way. No transition. Just boom! Swept away by the finality of her words, I quickly caved in. I hung up the phone on my mom. And I began to cry. And at the same time, I was angry. Audibly angry.

Luckily, at the time, I was sitting next to a lady who I call my spiritual grandmother. Shirley Johnson is her name. She graciously allowed me to wilt before her. She allowed me to grieve and vent in her car. I was angry. I was furious at my mother for her seemingly insensitive delivery of the news. And, oddly enough, I was mad at God. At that moment, I was actually confronted with something deeply tucked away in my spirit.

In that moment, it was revealed. Right there, I saw a prayer of my heart going unanswered. A prayer seemingly fell to the ground. And that realization revealed a bitterness I had toward God. I had all along been hoping for something to happen that was no longer going to happen.

The simple prayer that I once had was that I wanted to see my father at least once before he died. I wanted to let him know that I loved him. I wanted to let him know that I wasn't mad at him. And I wanted to ask him about his relationship with Jesus. I just wanted know if all was well with him. None of that was going to happen now....

The foggiest memory I have of my father was at another funeral in Jamaica for a relative from my maternal grandmother's side of the family. I honestly don't remember who died. (I think it was a great aunt). But I do remember the happiness that I felt because I got to visit my father on that trip. It was probably one of the happiest moments of my life. After all, I was with my dad. What could be greater than that?

I was only six years old, and up to that point, I had not a hint of a recollection of who my father was. So, everything about those few days was stellar. It was a weekend to remember in my young, impressionable mind. All the memories were so golden.

I remembered watching the movie *The Three Amigos* for the first time. I remembered drinking Milo, a chocolate malted drink. I remembered eating fried dumplings, plantains, and callaloo, which, in case you don't know, is a Jamaican spinach. I remember sleeping on the couch with the house pet, a kitten. What a comfort that feline was to me.

I remember my dad hot-wiring the vehicle we were in. I was fascinated by the fact that we did not need a key for the car to move. I thought, "This man is a genius. What a boss!" And I also remember spending time at the hospital visiting my grandmother. His mother. It was brief. She had cancer; a cancer that seemed peaceful at the time.

That's it. That's all I really can remember of my dad. At least that is what I can remember of him from a physical sense. Emotionally and spiritually, I have all kinds of memories that have to do with his absence.

That weekend was something near and dear to my heart. It was a beautiful and sacred weekend. It was such a contrast to another memory I had of my father, one in which he wasn't physically present. It was a memory I have of him over the phone. That was the day he didn't show up when he said he would. I was eight years old at the time. I remember it really well because at the end of it all, I cried myself to sleep.

My dad told me he was coming to visit me. He was coming to explain to me why things were the way they were. My heart was so full of expectation. But alas, it was not meant to be. I stayed up as long as I could, waiting for that bastard. The joke was on me. Pun intended.

I sat on the edge of that light blue Toyota Corolla. I sat for hours. I sat until day turned to night. Until night forced me to my bed. Until the Florida humidity had a competition with my sweat and with my tears. I have so few memories of him, but he had, and to a degree still has, such a profound effect on me. How is it that someone who was so absent in my life could have such an active effect, affect, and presence in my life?

It is the most irritating thing. Even at the age of 32, I still find myself riddled by the effects of an absent father. Father's Day is the worst day in the year. I just need to say that right here. For the last few years, that day has had a muted effect on me, mostly because I have been overseas during those times. But I have such a love-hate relationship with that day. It kills me.

On the best Father's Days, I have found it to be a wonderful way to honor God, my grandfather, and my male role models in the faith. On the worst Father's Days, well, let's just say my "feels" get wound up.

When I was in the 5th grade, we had a particular day in school that haunted me. We were working on a project. We were making tie-shaped cards for our respective fathers. Somewhere in the creation process, there was an epiphany that smacked me in the feels — right in my fifth-grade gut.

It was not the epiphany that I had hoped for, but nevertheless it hit me. The question dawned on me: Who am I making this card for? Right there and then, in class, I broke down and started crying. Bawling. Not that I was planning on it. But right there in class, I made a small scene. I didn't know how to deal with the reality of all that I was feeling at that time.

My teacher that year, Mrs. Lee, came over to console me. I was inconsolable at the moment. It hit me all at once. A vicious lie took hold of me. I realized that my father was not present in my life and that my mom wasn't as present as I would like. I felt like I was alone, and my parents did not love me or want me.

But more specifically the pain of not having a father to give a gift to bothered me. Mrs. Lee, knowing my family situation, reminded me that I had my grandparents present in my life. I had my grandfather to give my gift to. I remembered quickly responding to her. I told her it was not the same. I shouted, "It's not the same!"

Decades after this incident, I came to appreciate my grandfather's place in my life as well as other male mentors. And as I have gone further along on this journey, I have made strides to pay tribute to the many father figures God has placed in my life. Unfortunately, at that particular moment I realized that there was a seismic gap that belonged to my father: a hole that he had created. One that God is fixing, and others are helping to mend.

All of a sudden, a realization came over me. Something that I had not understood about life became clear. My situation growing up was different from the experiences of a lot of peers in school. Or at least that is what I assumed.

I instantly became naked and exposed to a sense of an unworthiness and a feeling of shame. Why didn't I have parents like everyone else? Where was my dad and why did I not live with both of my parents like most of peers at school and the people I saw on television? Why wasn't I placed in a family like the Huxtables? (It's a shame that the current Cosby scandal has tainted one of the beautiful images of black families in America, even if the image is fictional).

I have always lived in a two-tiered world as far as school is concerned. Academically, I was always a part of the gifted, honors, and advanced placement world, where people were lauded for their academic acumen and ability to score well on standardized tests. That world gave little honor to other forms of intelligence such as emotional, spiritual, or artistic expression. Let me not get too deep into that. I will save that for another time and/or book.

This was a world where many of the individuals in my class had both parents present in their lives; a world where parents worked vigorously on behalf of their children. They ensured that the legacy they built for themselves and their children would be perpetuated into the next generation.

While this took place, I also lived in a world filled with single-parent families and homes where the configuration did not follow the American Dream script. In this world, children emerged from those single-family homes and walked to the bus stop to catch the bus to school. In that world, limitations abound. It is a place where you were not expected to leave or go far from the city that you lived in. My actual neighborhood and home didn't quite follow this trend. But the tier system did exist.

In this two-tiered world, I found myself as a fifth grader, already realizing the pain of not having a father. I don't care what anyone tells you. Not having your parents, your mother and father present, will mess with you at some point or another in your life. It's such a basic element and need for a child's development. And at the very least, the societal advertisements and the "keeping up with the Jones family mentality will claw at your soul and make you question your upbringing."

A year after the aforementioned incident, the intensity of a missing dad became even more amplified for me. Early middle school was the setting, sixth grade, to be precise. It was a Saturday. I remember that tidbit because I was at Saturday school. If you are not familiar with such a day, then let me inform you.

Saturday school is the extra day of school you "earn" on the weekend when you did something bad during the regular school week. I am supposing my particular reason for being in Saturday school had something to do with my habit of talking excessively.

It was probably a combination of me being a class clown and hosting my own variety show during class time. I am sure that was the offense that landed me in Saturday school. It was rare for me to get in trouble for something like fighting. Hey, what can I say, I like to talk. Call me Gregarious Gary!

A day of Saturday school consisted of an early wake up, outdoor clean up, and sitting in an icy room doing dreadfully mindless "homework." Essentially, we were like the people you see in the orange jumpsuits cleaning the trash along the highways. We were the juvenile version doing the same thing for our middle school. I did my time, and so did everyone else. But what happened next was unexpected; something I had never wished for.

At the end of the day, I had to walk home. To get back home, I had to cross a bridge. That seems to be the grand metaphor of life. There is always a bridge to cross. Unfortunately, when I got on the other side of this bridge my heart, my mind, and my emotions were tampered with.

This bridge was a quintessential link to my middle school years. It was my pathway to home, to school, to recreational activities, and of course to my favorite local stores, Publix and Dollar General.

Shout out to the people who know the lavish sentimental experience of shopping at a Publix, *Where shopping is a pleasure*. There is no store quite like it for a person who grows up in the southeastern regions of America. (Although I have a skewed view of Publix now, because I question their labor and wage practices.) Anyway, back to the story.

When I began walking, I started out by myself. But as I continued, I could sense the presence of someone else behind me. It was another guy who used to go my school. I am pretty sure he had repeated a grade. He was, at the very least, two or three grades ahead of me. He was in high school at that time.

Unbeknownst to me, he had been following me, and he had been following me with an intent. And I turned around only to see that intent. A young man exposed. Have you ever had that feeling? You know, that sixth sense feeling when something is off? That moment before you turn around and you know it won't end like you expected it to end. That feeling of being preyed upon. That feeling of being unsafe. That feeling of being cornered. I had that feeling before I turned around.

Like predators do, he tried to corner me with conversation. He asked if me I wanted to go to the bathroom and to head back to the Publix we had passed. Hell no! That's what I said inwardly. And I wanted to say it outwardly, but instead, I was in shock. I just simply said no. And I quickly tried to get out of the situation. I would have given anything to just run out of my skin at that moment. What in world made this guy think that this was okay?

He then tried to pursue the situation further. He insisted that I come over to his house for video games. That wasn't happening.

That's when I decided to take a more proactive measure. You see, the bridge we were on was separated by two sets of three lanes. It had a median with flowers, palm trees, and a concrete barrier. And it had traffic that leisurely moved in both directions. As if I were playing a game of Frogger, I stepped boldly out into the lanes. Not worried of death, injury, or oncoming traffic, I quickly made my way across to other side.

I just needed to be on the other side. I wanted to be found in a place of security and freedom, away from the shadow of a predator. I simply needed to get out of there and be somewhere safe. When I was on the other side, I was confronted with a reality that I, in some degree, still face today. I was swallowed up with a dark and naked feeling. It was the overwhelming sense of not being protected.

Looming over me in that moment was a repeated phrase. More than anything, my mind and my heart sobbed this phrase, "I want my dad. Where is my dad? I want my dad. Where is my Dad?" I muttered those words under my breath, but I said them loudly and clearly in my heart.

Out of everything I could have thought of in that moment. That's all I was consumed with. He, my missing father, was the only person I wanted at that moment. It was visceral, instinctive, instant, and undeniable.

Some days I still feel like I am back on that bridge, just asking repeatedly, where is my father? From the negative sense, it happens most often when I hit moments of great insecurity, like when I can't seem to do the typical manly things that other men know how to do. Or when I can't seem to find breakthroughs in relationships with women. Especially in moments of rejection.

Or worse, when I can't seem to open my heart long enough. When I can't commit to something or someone long term because of my woeful inadequacies. When my fear of commitment, fear of rejection, and fear of neglect afflict me. These are moments where I put walls up to protect my heart. These are moments I really want to talk to my dad.

Fortunately, most days I am not on that bridge. Most days I find myself gently graced by the Holy Spirit, walking slowly with Jesus, and embracing God as my Heavenly Father. In those moments, I am not on that bridge. In those moments, the triune God is taking me to places that I would have never thought to go.

So, where is my father? This still remains the focal question for me, both from the negative and positive hues that surround it. This book is a recollection of a journey told in stories that surround that idea of searching for God and finding Him. The undergirding premise of this memoir is seeking and finding God in persons, places, and things, both expected and unexpected.

I view God as the father who boldly stepped in when my biological father couldn't and didn't. The great part about this is that God is often not where you and I expect Him, which makes the search much more enjoyable and unpredictable.

It has been written in the Holy Manuscript that, "if I seek Him, I will find Him when I seek with all my heart." That has been most of my life's aim. Seeking and finding God. Whether I try or not. That's who I am looking for. I will do so until the day I die.

It's hard to distinguish it at times, but my search for my earthly father seems to be inseparable to my search for my Heavenly Father. Although the primary focus of this book is on God the Father, I would be lying to you if this book wasn't also about my earthly father. This book is also an exposition of fatherlessness and Fatherhood. It's a huge theme in my life. After all, I found God the Father mostly because I couldn't find my biological one.

My earthly father is dead. However, before and after his death, I needed and wanted him in my life. And I have not been able to remedy the solution of this missing piece except for the graciousness of God. I am convinced that God knows how to remedy that which is missing in our lives.

I have found God in my search for my absent father. I couldn't find Ian Elroy Francis to be a constant figure of love, leadership, and guidance in my life, but I still found my Father. And He does these things so well. I pray that you will find Him in your own story as well. And I hope you will experience Him through reading my story, too! Thanks for joining me.

Now, let's continue with seeking and finding God in France...

CHAPTER 2

Silence

Silence. It is one of the hardest places to find God, and concurrently it is one of the easiest places to find him. It's a word, a place, a space, and a state of being all at once. It is an entity that is lightly blanketed in juxtapositions. The paradoxical element of silence is that it is always a moment's reach away; yet, is the furthest place to travel on earth on any given day. The journey to silence, however, is well worth it, especially when you find God in the silence.

My best experience with silence and solitude happened to me in a monastery in Taizé, France. I spent a week in silence with a small group of guys who were strangers. Each one of us traveled from all over the world to experience a pilgrimage of sorts. Each one of us had our story and reasons for choosing silence and solitude as our way.

It was a week of mixed emotions that I will never forget. Words can't express the encounter with God, myself, and the community I met during that time. To this day, I continue to draw upon that experience as my reminder of the value of practicing silence and solitude.

This trip was unique in that it was the first time I travelled alone overseas. It was incredibly daunting at first, mostly because it was lonely and risky. I went from sharing an exciting journey through Germany with about 20 people to traveling along a lonely road with myself, my thoughts, my journal, and my Father.

I got there by way of plane, train, and bus. After a 90-minute flight from Germany to France, I took a shuttle through the streets of Paris to the train station. After getting confused by my departure point, I took a long train ride into the countryside. Finally, my travel time concluded with a bus ride to Macon. From there, the Burgundy countryside and the hills of Taizé awaited. I almost got lost a thousand times on that trek. And I almost missed my connections to my next mode of travel at least 100 times. Despite the faux pas, it was wonderful. Getting lost and found was a joy unspeakable.

Disclaimer: I think I need to establish this truth about myself before we move forward. You have to understand this about me. *I really enjoy talking.* When say I like talking, I mean, a *lot*! So it may come as a shock to some of you that I willfully participated in a week of silence, but I did! And, parenthetically speaking, if I can do it, so can you.

I chose to do the week of silence as a part of a practicum for my graduate school program at Fuller Seminary. My time of silence was actually a small part of my graduate school endeavor. The practicum allotted me the beautiful opportunity to spend three weeks in Germany and three weeks in France.

In Germany, my practicum focused on a cross cultural leadership development trip with college-aged students. Most of them were members of a college group from Sierra Madre led by my friend and coworker Ryan Dahlstrom. In France, my practicum focused on an ethnographic study on the monastic community of Taizé. There, I studied the topics of solidarity, silence, and community. I also went there with soul-searching in my spirit.

The practicum also included a required element of vocational discernment. This is where the week of silence came in. I chose the week of silence as a means to connect with God and possibly find my vocational calling.

Each participant was assigned to a contact brother from the monastery to help us with our journey during the week of silence. Brother James was my contact brother. He was very dear to me during that time.

Now, I have to clear up one other thing before you call me a liar. It was a week of silence but to be fair, the time was technically interrupted twice in the week (and also for meal times). My silence was suspended for two 30 to 45-minute conversation sessions with Brother James. The time was used as a means to process my silence. It was their way of helping us process our experience. Boy, was there much to process.

One of the first things that I noticed about spending a week in silence is that is exhausting. I slept most of my first day in silence because I was so tired. Tired from what, you might ask? Well, for me, that's the whole surprise of it all. My first day and a half, I had to fight to be still. Everything within me had been on "go mode" for the last few weeks, months, and perhaps years. The actual process of deliberately slowing down and intentionally being still revealed that there were a thousand different things firing off in my mind.

My mind felt like an hourglass filled with cascading layers. Like Will Smith proclaims in the opening theme of *Fresh Prince of Bel Air*, little by little my life got turned upside down. Consequently, my senses were awakened to a peculiar reality. I noticed that I had an intense dialogue going on in my head and in my heart. I realized I had a lot of pain, unanswered questions, and frustrations that I had not previously dealt with. My thoughts were loud.

I also understood and felt the power of social media. All of a sudden my brain was freed from technology and a constant stream of information. This change caused my system to crash a little bit. No more '"likes." No more swiping. No more posting. Instinctively, my body did its best to help me with this overwhelming situation. Like someone who was drowning or someone whose blood pressure was too high, my body put me to sleep. It was a coping mechanism in full effect.

I wasn't the only one who had this experience, though. Brother James told me early in the week that this was normal for many people. My thoughts were like a waterfall. The cascade started with the most shallow and primal of thoughts. And then the thoughts carried me to the deep end and dropped me off there. Right away, I was drowning in myself. Fortunately, Brother James gave me great advice about what to do during my time in silence.

I was told to pick a spot on the map every day and walk to it. You see, there was a hand-painted map in the monastery. It was beautiful, surprisingly accurate, and perfectly measured to scale. The map showed neighboring villages and the churches that were in center of those towns. I was advised to pick spots so that I could walk and talk to God in my head along the way. And then when I arrived at a location, I should spend time drawing, writing in my journal, and praying.

These locations were typically a one- to two hour walk away from the monastery. The scenery along the route was breathtaking: nothing but rolling hills, streams, and pastures filled with cows, horses running free, and other grazing and free-ranged animals.

Each mini-pilgrimage was unique and equally peaceful and inviting.

In my everyday excursions, I would be greeted by the most luscious of vineyards and kindest of breezes in the world. Without fail, the locals would greet me affectionately. They seemed to know right away that I was in silence whenever we approached each other. They were probably used to encountering the many people who were on these pilgrimages.

My typical day of silence started out with me waking up with a piqued curiosity. I have a love affair with the morning when I am in a new place. I always have and I always will. Waking up at dawn is a delight to me, especially when I am in a foreign location. I usually wake with the desire to see the sunrise. However, the sensation is greater when you know that the view is going to be immaculate in the countryside. There's nothing like seeing the sun rise slowly atop the freshly setting dew that rests on the crests of the rolling hills of Taizé.

The air there always seemed to be crisp, and the sunrise and sunsets were always charming. Most of my mornings started that way. I needed no coffee because the scenery had a marvelous way of arousing my senses. (Besides, I don't like to drink coffee anyway.)

After my morning encounters, I would spend some time reading and writing as a means to connect with God. Then I would join my fellow silence seekers for breakfast. It was a peculiar part of the experience because we did all our meals in silence as a community. The added effect was having the experience with people you mostly did not know—*yet*. It was hella interesting.

This meal time was the only other time that we spoke. The phrase that we spoke together was our prayer. The Brother leading the prayer would say: *"Béni soit le seigneur Christ"* (Blessed is the Lord Christ). And we would respond *"qu'il soit benit toujours"* (may He be blessed in all times).

The only person to speak after that was the Brother who led our breakfast. It was very awkward at first. Imagine eating a whole meal in complete silence with about 15 other people. We would pass the buckets, utensils, food, cups, drinks, and desserts with no words. Gestures, facial expressions, and other forms of body language replaced talking. It was quite surreal, but it was a very pleasurable experience. The best part was when you wanted to laugh or say something silly but you couldn't.

When we ate, we sat outside in a semicircle. Depending on how we were arranged, or the occasion that was at hand, the seating lent itself to an extraordinary view of the countryside. Or sometimes we would sit at direct attention to the Brother who was leading our session. If we had chores, we would we stay after breakfast. If not, we would have some free time to do whatever we wanted. But once that time was over, we all returned to that spot. We would come back again to hear a scripture and/or a lesson.

It was a mesmerizing time because the Brother who was speaking had a captive audience. The fact that we couldn't converse made it a definite one-way street of listening. Whatever was taught was clearly delivered without reply or response. There wasn't even an "amen" to compliment his teachings.

I would often spend my time before lunch doing one of several things. Either I would hand-wash my clothes, or I would spend time trying to replicate the Taizé Sacramental art that I saw in the community and in my room. Or I would try to read one of my required seminary readings and write in my journal.

Lunch followed the same format as breakfast, except that I had kitchen duty after the meal with a group of three fellows from our quiet community. This, my friends, was powerful. To this date, I have never had such a dynamic, unique demonstration of teamwork. With gestures and nonverbal pleasantries, we quickly formed an assembly line to clean pots and pans. We would sometimes hum to ourselves as we worked. I don't know if that counts as speaking, but we did it anyway.

One of my cleaning companions was from the African nation of Chad; another was from Hungary; and the third was from Croatia. We revealed our home nations to each other at the end of the week. But before we found that out, we spoke without words. We grew close to each other in the common brotherhood of silence.

Lunch was followed by my time of walking. I went from village to village and visited church after church. Each of these churches was predominantly empty. They possessed more of a museum feel than a living space of worship. However, in the absence of people and activity, each place possessed an indelible quality and a special message from God. Sometimes, all I heard from those visits was, "I love you", or, "Show others my love."

Each evening, we concluded with dinner, and we joined the larger group of pilgrims for prayer, silence, chanting, and acts of solidarity. The larger group included 3,000 other people on pilgrimage. Taizé, outside of the times of silence can sometimes be a rather noisy place. It can be a tough place to try to maintain a week of silence. Walking through the larger area was very tempting because everyone there was free to chat, unlike us.

In short, this was my way of life for a week. I relished it, I loved it, and sometimes I hated it. But mostly, I embraced it — wholeheartedly.

The silence had marvelous effects on me. I came away from the experience feeling that silence reveals everything. Well, not everything. But many things! Many things are surfaced through silence and solitude. This duo has a tendency to reveal the hidden things. The things that are lodged in our souls.

The solitude, the aloneness with God, facilitates the moments where God can speak to you and me clearly. When there are no words, people, and technology to compete with, all of sudden you are left with yourself and God. It can be daunting. Silence is the confrontation and the conversation that your soul and your God have been waiting to have with you. For me, it was just that. The things I have been meaning to say and needing to hear only happened in silence.

I don't how much I am going to share of these moments with you, mostly because that time of silence did something to me that words cannot describe. Also, I don't know what will be appropriate to share with you. I'm currently trying to learn to manage my boundaries better. I tend to go deep pretty quickly, and, consequently, I tend to be burned pretty quickly.

But here is what I can say about my week in silence:

- It was when I was completely still and silent that God distinctly gave me directions for His life — my life intertwined with His. It was in those moments that He gave me His plan. He did it during that time. And He continues to do it now.

- Silence revealed the evil in my heart. You don't know how much sin is in you until you meet with an Almighty God and realize who you are in comparison to Him. I know that sin is an unpopular notion in our day and age, but it still exists. Silence and solitude take away the noise that tries to shout over God's still small whispers to us. And in those moments God is seen for who He is: Holy.

- Silence reveals pain. That's probably the reason most people avoid it. The longer I stayed in silence, the more easily I saw my wounds and the things I was running from. But the more I chose not to run away, the more easily God would heal my wounds. In choosing silence, I chose reality.

- Silence reveals truth. Silence reveals things as they are and not as we wish them to be. In the silence, I saw things plainly. Nothing had a chance to masquerade itself because silence doesn't tolerate dishonesty. Whether good or bad, I could not help but notice the world within and around me in its truest form.

- Silence reveals joy. The most simple and pure things are elevated in silence. All of a sudden, nature sounded like a beautiful chorus. Simplicity became a friend of mine in that time. A zest for the seemingly mundane sprang up like a well within me as things became apparent. Silence stoked the fire for the natural things that brought me joy in life.

- Silence reveals God's secrets. It is in the still moments that God chooses to show a unique part of Himself. And without a doubt, a unique part of myself opened up to God. If you ever want to know how God really feels about you, let silence, and its companion solitude, show you the way to His heart.

One of the most dynamic things about the week of silence is that it is done communally. For an entire week, you become close to people without using words. You share the most common, basic modalities of life. You eat meals, you clean, you listen to God, and you share the same space of solitude and silence.

And then, you have that first moment to speak to each other. Who are these people I have done kitchen chores with? I feel like I know them, but I don't even know most of their first names. This was the intriguing part. The sacred space created a bond, a closeness, and kindred friendship. Something of great depth was created in an unspoken form of unity.

And then you get hit with the rude awakening. Reality sets in. You realize that many of the people with whom you experienced silence are from different parts of the world. You don't even share the same spoken language, and you become dumbfounded and bewildered. How was it that I got closer to people in silence than I could when speaking to them? The language barrier presented more of a hurdle than silence did. And it taught me a power that silence had: silence is a form of intimacy.

By the end of my time in silence, you would have thought I would be eager to talk. But the opposite occurred. I had no real desire to talk. I found it difficult. My bubble was popped. My connection with God and with others had been interrupted. I had to relearn how to navigate relationships in a world of noise, distraction, and words — both useful and useless. I began to resent the sounds around me because they seemed so reckless and unintentional.

Although I could speak, I found myself trying my best to limit my words. Silence had started to train me to be better in the art of listening. Pauses and hesitations in conversations were welcomed, instead of filling in the blanks with vocalized uneasiness. I became determined to keep silence as a staple part of the rhythm in my life. Although very difficult, I try to insert it in the pockets and expanses of my daily routine. Even if that means putting it as a reminder on my smartphone.

I honestly think silence is the quickest way to find my Father. But I have to admit, I am often scared of being still and silent. I am often plagued with fearful questions. What if God wants me do something I don't want to do? What if He shows up in way I can't bear?

And I am often "delfrightened" about silence. (I know you like that word.) I am quite often caught in a tug of war of being *delighted* and *frightened* about the intimate God I find in the silence. A love-hate, push-pull dynamic occurs. My soul screams in delight to be in the presence of God, but my flesh is dying to run away, longing to be caught up in trivial, worldly desires.

The best example of this dynamic is finding God in my chair. It is a very special place that I meet my Father. It is a special place that I love and hate at the same time. However, it is a bit early to talk about the chair. You have to wait until chapter 6 before I feel comfortable enough to share that with you. And let's be real. I am not ready to talk about the chair yet. But when I do, please be gracious. For now, let's talk about one of my greatest failures and greatest celebrations! These are the perfect places to seek and find God daily.

CHAPTER 3

Friends and Failures

Failures tend to reveal God in very unique ways. In some occasions, I am convinced that failures are better than victories, especially the failures in which I flop completely. For example, when I just completely take a trip down Loserville, it's in those moments that God seems to be revealed to me more than ever. It is as though another part of his Father nature is put on display.

I guess it's that whole thing about His grace being perfected in our weakness. God sure knows how to love us at our lowest points. Throughout my life, He has had a knack for celebrating me, and, I presume, you at the oddest and most unexpected times. God in his most precise judgments definitely issues punishments — consequences if you will — that I indeed deserve because of my sins. (And you, too; you're not so perfect, either.) However, He simultaneously tends to offer us party gifts when we least expect them.

One of His favorite methods of celebration is grace and mercy. It's when He gives you and me things that we don't deserve, and he holds back the things (we think) we do deserve. It's those moments where I can't earn or deserve anything but instead I just receive the love God is giving me and the power to overcome. He is a great Father in that way....

One of the most humiliating moments of my life happened in the spring of 2013. This event also resulted in one of the most mercy-filled, grace-filled moments in my life. At the time I was living in Altadena, California with seven other roommates. Yes, you read that correctly. When you hear those stories of people living like sardines because the rent is so expensive in southern California, believe it. I couldn't have afforded to live in that part of the country without those seven other people.

The configuration of the house was something out of a SoCal sitcom made from our own doing. Technically speaking, the house only had three rooms. So, you must be wondering how in the world we fit that many people in this place. I'm glad you asked.

Well, there were Jordan and Joey, a pair of guys who lived in the front room of the house. Joey moved to Lebanon and Gabi promptly took his place, but Jordan remained. Jordan was a lively character, to say the least. My roommate and I, Curtis, lived in the middle portion of the house with a bunkbed configuration in our room. Our setup was temporary because Curtis would leave in a few months to become a married man. Then, I had a room to myself until Zack came a few months later.

Dan had his own room with the best space-to-person ratio. Lucky duck. He was set up in the backroom. He had the most luxurious space of us all. And then, we fashioned together another room for Aaron, a room that was originally a breakfast nook. Please don't tell the landlord that we did this. Technically, the lease was only for four people.

When I say we fashioned a room, what I mean is that we placed a futon in that beast and called it good. It literally was a nook, not a room. Aaron, also known as Boo or Blaaron (a combination of the words black and Aaron), occupied that space. We had another roommate, who also was named Aaron, who was of the Caucasian persuasion, so he was the Whaaron (white Aaron) of the household!

Back to the story at hand. If you are decent with math, then you have recognized that my math does not add up properly. I mentioned there were eight occupants, including me, at this particular location. Thus far I have only mentioned six of the people who lived there.

Well, we had two other roommates, Jacob and Aaron (Whaaron), both of whom lived in their vans. Yes, *vans*, or hippie mobiles, as some might say. They were state-of-the-art hippie mobiles, though. Jacob lived in the driveway parallel to our home, and Aaron lived in his van inside our garage. Talk about efficiency.

Now, did I mention that we had to share two bathrooms, one shower, and one kitchen? That is one shower and one kitchen for eight guys. Just imagine all of the joys and sorrows that this set-up brought us. I have to say though, it worked for the most part. It was an once-in-a-lifetime experience. Key word: once.

Half of our house went to the same graduate school at Fuller, and that particular half also worked at the same after-school program, The Neighborhood Urban Family Center. It was a program that focused on tutoring, holistic growth, and academic help for underserved and underprivileged children in kindergarten through 5th grade. Underserved and underprivileged are the politically correct terms for those experiencing poverty *and* who happen to be predominantly brown skinned and/or of the Latin persuasion. The children, by the way, were some of the best kids on the planet. I absolutely loved being with them. And I dearly miss them. Children are gifts from God.

So, essentially, we had a slew of atypical theologians, pastor-like people, mission-minded homies, a techie/social media guru, music artist, and business-like persons all under one roof. We were men who had hearts to change the world while co-existing amicably in an unorthodox community.

To say the least, this was an interesting place to live. It was definitely an interesting and challenging time for me to live there. While living there, I worked as a site director for the aforementioned afterschool program. It was one of the most fulfilling jobs that I have had to date, but it was a part-time job, so keeping up financially was very challenging for me. After all, we lived in a typical Southern California city.

I was struggling to make it in the California dream. And then struggle got real. *Too* real.

It was 2am in the morning. Everyone was asleep in the house, when all of a sudden I heard banging on the windows and flashlights dancing in my eyes. I also could hear the commotion of a guy calling my name.

It was a cold morning —freezing by Southern California standards. This was during one of those wacky cold spells that hit the area from time to time. The guy who was calling my name was the repo man. He had come to get my car. A combination of bad choices, miscommunication, limited finances, and bad timing caught up to me.... Snuck up on me....Smacked me!

Right there in the frigid drafty morning, I woke up disillusioned. I was jolted from my pleasant sleep and confronted by an unnecessarily rude man who was paired with an ultra-sweet, petite woman. They were chaining up my car. My poor dark blue Malibu — Mali was her name —was being taken away from me. And so was my pride.

The man was maniacal in his disposition. He made me feel, figuratively, like fecal matter. Never had I felt the way I did at that moment. I felt like I was being castrated. I didn't feel like a man. I felt subhuman. I am pretty sure my man card was on the dashboard when they drove away.

It was just a car, right? Just an object; an inanimate product. A conglomeration of plastic, metal, and leather. But it hit me hard. I had failed. It was another one of those moments I wish I had my earthly father present, even if it was a moment of being lectured by him. Or a moment where I could have called and said, "Dad, I messed up real bad today." Maybe it could have been a moment we would laugh about years down the road.

How in the world did I get to a place that my car was repossessed? I felt so irresponsible and so vulnerable at the same time. My housemate Dan asked me how I was doing a few minutes after they left. I had no words; just a look of despair. In a fit of emotional exhaustion, I went to bed. I was hoping my Father would bring new mercies in the morning.

Losing the car changed the dynamics of everything I did. Right away, getting to work was a challenge. Getting to school was a challenge. Life in general was a challenge. Nevertheless, God worked wonders with the situation. I sincerely would never change what happened because God was present through it all. I found God to be Immanuel —"God with me" — during that time.

I bought a bicycle to get around. It was a steal of a deal. And boy did that change my worldview. My bike's name was Cali. It was short for Caliente. It was the name of the bikes in that particular series. It was a hot red Schwinn road bike. It was a sexy beast. (As I am writing this, I realize I have a thing about naming and nicknaming things and people. I guess it's just one of the ways that I show love.)

It's a whole different world when you have to ride a bike to get to work, get groceries, travel through downtown LA, or do any typical task. When hills are involved it's a joy to the soul. *Sarcasm alert!* Guess, what? Guess where I lived? Uphill! The beauty and grace granted to me on those bike rides humbled me, though. Some of my best conversations with God came during those rides. There's nothing like talking to God when your bike chain pops off in the middle of your 30-minute, mostly downhill commute to work.

I also had to use the public transit system a whole lot. I genuinely loved it. I enjoyed the pace of it. Everything in my life slowed down. I had to plan things out much more now. I had the opportunity to talk to people and share life. There was a space to grieve the commonality and differences of our walks. During those wonderful conversations, we voiced complaints, counseled each other, and chatted about life. Of course, the other side of the coin is that the public transit was deathly slow whenever I was running late. Probably the most stressful times in LA were accompanied with an off-schedule bus coupled with a rushed, sweaty ride to work. (Sigh).

In the transitions between places, I had some authentically beautiful interactions with people experiencing poverty. I found myself involved frequently in priceless moments of exchange. I got to give, and others gave to me. My favorite of these exchanges was when I was returning home from one job and trying to make it to another. I met a gentleman, who on first glance, appeared to be homeless and, perhaps, an alcoholic. Looks can be deceiving, though.

Although I have had many relationships and interactions we with people experiencing homelessness, this one sticks out in my memory a whole lot. It reminded me of a fellow I had met in Skid Row a few months back. (We will talk about him and Skid Row later on.) If I were to just go by appearances I would have said he was in much more dire need of assistance than I was. But one thing I have definitely learned throughout life is that I quite often need to suspend judgement. I have learned to do a better job of reprioritizing the status quo when it comes to first impressions and first encounters.

This man went out of his way to help me that day. He spotted me right away. His name was Andrew and he insisted that he was going to help me out that day. He had a beard, dark skin, and voice that had a sing-song rhythm to it. Not in a Caribbean way. Rather, he spoke with a beat poet tempo. His talking voice sounded like he was going to deliver wisdom through spoken word or maybe a song.

He showed me where to place my bike on the rack in front of the bus. Then he promptly told me, "You are going to be my brother today! After all, you are my brother. And I am going take care of you. Don't you dare worry about paying for your bus fare! I've got your change."

He was insistent. I was definitely living the broke as a joke life, but it felt like Jesus was talking to me through this man. I complied and we sat during that 20 minute stretch of time and it was beautiful. We chatted about various topics in life. He mentioned something about his recovery group and how God showed up in mysterious ways. The change he gave me, both figuratively and literally, was a precursor to other changes in my life. Most of them were unexpected. Most of them were gifts in the midst of utter failure.

Without a car, and no foreseeable future of having one, I became more dependent on others. (Sigh). My friendships grew to a different place. I had to lose a lot of my independence and control during that period of time. All of a sudden I became ultra-aware of the care and sincerity of people. I fell into a wonderful world that was fresher than it had ever been: a world called interdependence. I became cognizant of a beautiful world of learning how to receive and give.

Conversations that would never happen, happened. Especially where it concerned my volleyball friends. People like Nasim, Shon, and Johnny graciously helped me out in my rocky times. Between conversations, rides to work and play, and unexpected visits, my heart was full. And then my heart became overfilled. There was too much love to handle. It spilt over when one of my volleyball friends genuinely surprised me. Her name was Lauren.

Funny enough, she didn't play volleyball. In fact, her husband Tony was the one that played volleyball. Lauren typically came to the Meetups in a sporadic fashion to come cheer him on, hang out with some of us from the group, and of course be her awesome self.

On her very first visit to the park we met each other through the sidelines. Apparently my infectious laughter and on-court (and sideline) commentary was amusing to her. During one of the times I wasn't playing, we sparked up several conversations about changing the world. We laughed a lot and challenged each other on the depth that humanity could reach in loving people. With this, we became instant friends.

You have to understand Lauren's nature. She oozed compassion and care. She didn't back down from helping others. And she sought to bring comfort to those whom she loved. She didn't know me for a very long time but upon hearing my dilemma of my car she sprang into action. She decided to throw a Jack and Jill party for me. At the time I had never heard of such a thing. Have you ever heard of Jack and Jill party?

It turned out to be an awesome event. She, along with her good friend Ally, threw me an epic party to raise funds to get my car back. Epic! The event was powerful in that it combined several, different spheres of my life all into one place. My volleyball friends, church friends, grad school friends, work friends, and housemates all collided together for a celebration. We had the kind of celebration you want from people you love before you die- not at your funeral.

I really didn't deserve that event. It was completely my fault that my car got repossessed, but the mercy and grace showed to me that night was palpable. It was tears-to-your-eyes worthy. There were musical acts. One that was done by roommate Gabi. He sang Frank Ocean's "Thinking about you," wooing the crowd and the ladies in particular. At the time he was trying out to be on show *The Voice*. So you know them vocals were on point.

There were games, great food, giveaways, and dancing. There was so much laughter that my soul ached in a good way. The setting was beautiful and the people were even better. We didn't actually raise all the funds to completely get my car back. Although the money raised did make a serious dent in the debt that I had accrued during that time, I actually didn't have a car again until almost two years after. Consequently, trusting God and others became more than normative for me.

There was, however, a larger dent made. It was the dent created in my heart; a crater nestled in my soul. My Father carved out a space for mercy and grace deep within. My parameters on loving people, unifying people, identifying with brokenness, giving and receiving grace and mercy ... were altered forever.

I learned many powerful lessons from that time. And I continue to do so from other moments in life. My Father is constantly teaching me simple, tangible, and necessary truths. This is no surprise because I have always been accustomed to learning by experience. These moments of learning, however, are not from my own doing but rather from divine inspiration and key people in my life.

As I reflect on my life I have to mention one of those key people. She was an elderly woman with a youthful soul. If you met her you would understand what I mean. Walk with me a little bit more and I will tell you about her. Her name is Granny.

CHAPTER 4

Granny

Granny. She lived to be 105 and half years old. She was my great-grandmother. She was a grandmother to many, but a mother of two. She was a daughter; the eldest out of a family of 14. Now, that's a lot of kids! Back then, they didn't have television. So, I am guessing they made children in their spare time. She was kind. She was extremely entrepreneurial in nature. She was magnetic. She was also a figure of hope and inspiration to the masses. But personally, she was...

Seeking and finding God can oftentimes be an experience that happens through key people in one's life. It's the time spent with these special people that teach you life's most essential lessons. It's the direct and indirect lessons that such persons give you that show you how to live one's life meaningfully and mindfully. And if you are lucky enough, you experience God's presence and love in the process.

My great grandmother was a person who embodied such sentiments. My family and I affectionately called her by the title of Granny, but you can call her Adassa Henry because that was her given name. However, if you get close to my family and me, you can call her Granny too!

Even at this point in my life, at the age of 33, I have spent more of my life with her present, then with her absent. That is shocking to me. I am exponentially grateful to have had her in my life for 28 years. It's so rare to hear someone one live to that age, let alone to have them be a part of your own family. My maternal side of my family had the wonderful experience of having 5 generations of family present at the same time while she was alive. It was heartbreaking and bittersweet when she died. She went home to be with the God she so desperately loved.

When I was younger, hanging out with Granny was often my place of comfort. In her room, by her bedside, I learned a lot about Our Father and a lot about character. Her room was a place of peace for me when I was frustrated with my grandmother (her daughter), with life in general, or when my day was bad. And it was place of solace and celebration, to honor what God did throughout that day. Without fail, praise and thanksgiving were a common occurrence that happened in that space.

The edge of her bed was an altar where I confessed and learned to talk to God candidly. On my knees I learned to pray and I understood God to be real and relevant. No time of my life has a comparison to it. We talked a lot about God in that room. We also read a lot of the Bible in that room. When I say *we* read, I mean *I* would read aloud, Granny would listen, and then we would discuss God's truths together.

She had this HUGE, tan-colored Bible with golden lettering and golden trim on the outside. I remembered the golden trim in particular, because I would retrace it with my fingers in a methodical fashion in between thoughts and conversations. Tucked away in the Bible there was always a bookmarker. Whether legitimate or illegitimate, there was always a place marker for a particular scripture to study. The illegitimate bookmarks were often the programs and bulletins from the previous weeks at church. During those days we went to Calvary Assembly of God for church.

That Bible she had was a beast! It was built to last through an apocalypse. It was the kind of Bible that was designed for senior citizens with vision issues. The large print was astounding to me as a kid. I felt like the letters engulfed me as I read them aloud. Each page struck me as so profound, when I read them with Granny.

Our ritual was to spend time with each other, just before she went to bed. Or on the rare occasion, just before I went to bed. We would read scripture, discuss a little bit of its meaning, and end our time in prayer. Both of us would also take time to pray for each other, our family, and our personal concerns. Quite often, in our times we would also include singing hymns. To this day I can hear the song, *Bring in the Sheaves* once in while in the back of my mind.

The time would officially end with me giving Granny a gentle hug and saying I love you. Then, I would typically make sure the blinds and windows were closed in her room. The blinds were the type where you had to pull a lever. She sometimes didn't have the strength to do it herself.

What followed next was the ritual to make her room comfortable. I would turn on her night light or light her kerosene lamp so the room wasn't so dark. She was old school when it came to lighting her room. I bet you have never seen or heard of a kerosene lamp? She was the only one I knew that used it. That lamp was something right out of an antique road show. That thing must be worth a thousand dollars by now.

I also saw Granny's room as a place of refuge and formation of my identity. She was one of the few people who understood me as a kid and generally as a person. In fact, she was the first person who took me to church regularly, but more importantly she was the first to recognize and tell me of God's calling in my life. At a very young age I had a very close knit relationship with God. Granny was the primary person that affirmed and confirmed this by telling me some important words God spoke about me. Her words rang powerful. They lead me closer to God.

She told me that the "The Spirit" woke her up one day. It was during the school week, as I was participating in my early elementary days. I want to say that I was in third grade at the time. I'm not for sure though. She was prompted to look outside the window. There I was with my backpack. She saw me walking to school that day and God told her, "You see that young man. I have marked Him for my purposes."

Words like that can have a profound effect on a person. For me, those words propelled me further into the direction that Life is taking me now. Those words continued to remind me of who I am when I don't see myself clearly. They helped me, and still help me, remember that my life is not my own. My life is a part of a bigger story.

It wasn't just the words she said. It was the accompanying actions. She did the combination of words and actions so well. Granny taught my family a peculiar phrase that I have never been able to shake. Whenever I say it, in my mind I can hear a collective sigh of agreement within me. It's the sigh that every family member and friend who knows Granny would understand. This phrase is ingrained in our DNA.

She spoke constantly of these words, "Manners rule the world." Whether consciously or unconsciously, I have shaped much of my life based on this phrase alone. But what does it mean? Well, the odd thing about it is that the phrase is best understood in practice. It is a phrase attached to experience. It is more of something that is caught rather than taught. But since I am here with you in this moment, let me do my best to relay the principles of the phrase.

Manners rule the world. It's actually quite a subversive thought. It's to see the world from a different angle. For the most part our world runs quite different from being mannerable. In fact, much of the world's interactions are based on indecent acts of incivility. The truth is that the uncivil, the unmannerly, most often rule the world. Cutthroat rules the world. Selfishness rules the world.

So, the first thing to realize is that the phrase directs the hearers to live life opposite of the prevalent trend of rudeness. In effect, my great grandmother taught me to subversive from a young age. She was teaching me to be rebellious and revolutionary- in a good way.

Manners rule the world meant to do all of your affairs with care, honoring people first above their capabilities, using loving language, and respecting others even if you don't know them. All people are to be respected no matter their background or how they treat you. It wasn't being a doormat but it was approaching all encounters with civility, proper decorum, and delivering respect.

Now, don't get me wrong, this didn't mean that she enjoyed everyone she met. Let's just say she was diplomatic. It was quite evident if she didn't like you. And she didn't mince words if she didn't approve of your behavior or actions. Nonetheless, she simply didn't let these things affect her. She had an uncanny way to show impeccable respect to people she didn't know. From the first contact she had with a person, they were locked into a moment of honor in some way. It was her way of doing life, business, and interacting with the greatest to the least in our Western world caste system of society.

When you reach the age of 90+ you get away things that other people could never get away with. You are allowed to say what you want. You automatically command the attention and respect of all who enter your presence. It's quite a wonderful perk that comes with royal seniority. I hope I grow old enough to experiment and experience this.

My great grandmother had a wonderful way of commanding this type of attention. She enforced it with an unassuming gesture called the "Granny Grip." That is what I called it anyways! On the surface it looked like a handshake but in reality it was a ploy for an encounter of truth. Once my Granny shook your hand you were locked in for something powerful. She would shake your hand first. Then she would shake your mind. Your soul would be shaken soon after.

She would either lean in close to you or you would lean in close to her. With eyes focused on your heart she spoke with intentionality. What followed next were whispered words of wisdom. Some people left the encounter with their tails tucked in between their legs. In that moment she probably spoke something that convicted the listener. She most likely admonished them and highlighted an area in which they can improve or change.

Others would spring up with excitement. Their shoulders would straighten up. They found new purpose and direction. In such an incident Granny spoke words that assured and affirmed them in their current state of affairs. I am convinced God spoke through her prophetically. Especially, when she sat on the veranda of the house I grew up in. I can't tell you how many times people encountered the Granny Grip there. Each one left their time with Granny as a different and bettered human being.

There was another element to the Granny Grip. There was the generosity also found in the Grip. You never knew what surprise might end up in your hand as she held you captive for a few minutes. Granny was famous for always having something to give. Just in the same she would enforce the Granny Grip, she would also enforce the "Pentecostal handshake." It's the type of handshake that results in gaining a gift of sorts. (If you have been around certain church folks long enough, you will understand this much clearer.)

Most often Granny gave people "sweeties"- little pieces of candy. I know these candies very well because I bought many of them from the Dollar Store down the road. Or sometimes the handshake would result with money for the receiver. *Or* she would disappear into her room to find something random to give to you. The whole point was to make sure that each person never left empty- handed. Words of encouragement, acts of kindness, and intentional moments of affirmation were part and parcel. It was just who she was. And to a degree, it was something I aspire to pass on. I hope this would be a legacy in the making.

To Granny everyone was family. And every person I saw around her treated her that way. I have never met a person who was claimed by so many people as their own grandmother. Everyone beloved Granny as if she was their very own Granny. Sometimes I wanted to be selfish and remind them, "Hey, let's not get too comfortable here, she is *actually* my great grandmother." (I said that with a smirk)

This familial nature Granny possessed was also present in my neighborhood. The neighborhood I grew up in was set up like a cultural utopia. Across the street our neighbors were Puerto Rican, next door they were Venezuelan, on the other side they were Canadian. And then there were more on the street who were Jamaican, African American, Cuban, German, and other ethnicities. It is no doubt that I grew up with an affinity for cultural diversity because my neighborhood displayed it.

My great grandmother solidified my love affair with other cultures and people groups by her treatment of people. I learned it by the way she interacted with our neighborhood. Her and my grandmother took care of many of our neighbors kids. We always had some baby, child, or little cousin being taken care of in the house. Whether they looked like me in skin complexion, or not, they became a part of our family.

Many times these children became Jamaican by osmosis because of their acquired diet and language. Many of them ate the same things we did and spoke the way we did. Every child in our household had to eat porridge at some point. This is *very* Jamaican. And each one of them had a little bit of the Jamaican patois stuck in their lingo.

Speaking of food. Cooking with Granny was a treat. When I was a young boy the kitchen with Granny was like a Bob Marley or Beres Hammond song being played on a record in the background. Everything about those times made me feel good inside. Even the moments that seemed scratchy had a good feel to it. My favorite part was making Jamaican desserts. Whether it was toto, gizzada, sweet potato pudding, rum cake, or bread pudding- it didn't matter. What mattered was that we were doing it together and at the end I got to lick the bowl. Haha!

Hands down, the best dessert we made together was coconut drops. I liked this one the most because it involved the most traditional elements in my mind. We used a Dutch pot to cook the coconuts, ginger, and brown sugar. I can smell it in my mind right now. What I loved the most was the way we set the coconut drops to cool. My great grandmother would send me outside to fetch some banana leaves. This for some reason was one of the most soothing things in my soul. It was so simple. It was so traditional. And I loved it!

Carefully and meticulously we would lay out the banana leaves. With love and care we would place each drop on a leaf. We would keep going until the pot was almost empty. Whatever was left was mine to scrape, to lick, and enjoy.

I have to thank God for Granny. Without her in my life I am worried that my future would have been abysmal. I had many ingredients in my life that could have taken me to a more negative turn. I needed someone like her in my life to give me some well-placed guidance and hope. She provided that and more. Not just for me but for many others. She was the kind of person I needed to have in the beginning of my life to set me on positive track for life.

Granny's funeral, along with my father's funeral, had a profound effect on my memory and life in general. There was this one moment I can't forget. Just before she was about to be put into the ground. We had a matriarchal/patriarchal Old Testament moment. It felt like we reading the last chapter of Genesis, which was fitting because I just finished that book weeks earlier.

I don't exaggerate this. I am not speaking in hyperboles. As Pastor Stephen spoke the words, "ashes to ashes, dust to dust. So you came, and so you will return," the wind kicked up in a dramatic fashion. It was powerful and poignant. It was undeniable that someone extremely vibrant and influential left the earth.

... Who was Granny to me? She was someone who loved God and understood her purpose. To me she was someone who truly understood me as I was. And now she was gone. What do you do when that happens?

A very important way to understand the ways of God is to respect, honor, and listen to the words and actions of the elders of our society. Especially, those who have lived meaningful God-centered lives. Such persons have paved the way for us and given us the necessary warnings, admonishments, and lit paths that we need to succeed.

The art of appreciating the eldest people in our communities has grown to be very outdated in our current society. I wish this were not so. The disparity of communication of the youngest and the oldest is problematic. And I find it to be a detriment to our overall progress.

I believe if we want to understand the ways of God we might find it in the ways of the eldest in our society. We need to find the oldest people we know and simply listen to them. Listen to their stories. Hear the beautiful and reckless changes that have happened in our world. Let them teach you and I the ways of the Lord. In this we might find that we hear God in their old souls.

CHAPTER 5

A Storm

In less than a week we would be back in the United States. At that moment, we were leaving the Mokan Island. We were heading back to the mainland. We were returning to the peaceful fishing village of Ranong. We were saying our salutations to the humble and loving community of Mokens. And then the rains came.

It was a "smallish" storm. We were told it would pass on soon. We would be on our way once it blew over. The torrential downpour came in quickly and thoroughly. The heavenly outpouring left the same way in which it came. After waiting it out, we gathered our things and said our second and last goodbyes. The sky, surprisingly, cleared up. All that was left were small patches of grey in the distance. Nothing too distressing though, but you have to always remember, the ocean can be a fickle place. That's something that we would learn quickly. A lesson we would never forget.

We waited out the storm. We had dodged a dicey situation on the waters. Now we were back on track for smooth sailing. Or so we thought...

Ever since I was a little kid, I have always wanted to go to Thailand. My fascination with the country, the culture, and the people started in fourth grade. My initial affinity for this nation came from a book report I did in Mrs. Lee's class. Thailand was the country I chose to share with my classmates. I have fond memories doing a show-and-tell project with a picture book of facts to my peers. I can still see the book in my mind. It had a picture of a beautiful temple and the words Thailand in shiny lettering.

Everything about my fourth grade study on Thai culture was riveting to me. And I was convinced that I must visit this enchanted place. This desire was further emboldened by a project we did the following year in Mrs. Lee's class.

Mrs. Lee was the best. She always did the most intriguing projects. I was in her gifted class for fourth and fifth grade. In fifth grade, we did this amazing international traveling project. Each student had to bring in a stuffed animal with a fanny pack. These stuffed animals were sent on a journey around the world. In the fanny packs there were postcards and directions to its receivers.

Each recipient was instructed to leave a postcard or a note of their journey. They were then told to pass on the stuffed animals as they went about their travels. Near the end of the year the last person in possession of the stuffed animal was supposed to send it back to our school at Sunshine Elementary.

Not everyone received their animals. I was rather fortunate. My dog, which was a knock-off version of Charlie Brown's Snoopy, returned home to me. He had been everywhere. He went on business trips, vacations, and celebrations. He went to Cozumel, other parts of Mexico, to India, and of course- Thailand! In a peculiar way, this without a doubt, settled it for me. In my heart I knew I would go to Thailand someday. And guess what? I got the chance to go there two years ago. It was more than just a trip. It was a childhood dream being fulfilled. Another gift from my Father.

For six and half weeks I had the greatest opportunity to travel to Southeast Asia with a small team of nine. Most of our time was in Thailand but in the middle of our trip our team spent ten days in Cambodia. We ran the gambit on experiences in both countries. We flew a ton, rode on tuk-tuks (automated rickshaws), participated in medical clinics, and partnered with life-empowering projects. We learned some of the language, hung out with elephants, ate the best food in the world for cheap, and made friends with all types of people. We even had a near death experience. I never dreamt that we would die there. However, the end of the trip definitely tested that idea. There are somethings you just can't plan for. And there are somethings you just have to accept once they happen.

... Like I said before, we had dodged the first storm. Little did we know, we were entering into another storm. One that was much bigger and much more threatening. We were in a small to medium size boat that had about 18 passengers on it. It was a long-tail boat. It's the type of boat that is reminiscent of when you think of Thailand, tourism, and river travel. It's the boat type that has the motor suspended on a mount. It has a long pole with the propeller suspended further back in the water. The pole could swivel with a 180 degree radius.

When we first took to the open waters it didn't seem like there was much rain coming our way. That changed promptly. Fifteen minutes into our travels we started getting a light drizzle. Just some sprinkles we hoped. The rain started lightly. People we were fine at first. Many opted not to use their rain gear in the beginning because the showers were so light. Without warning, the rains just kept coming.

Steadily we received more and more drops. These drops started to have greater weight to them. This is when the ponchos started to come out in full force. People were getting soaked.

Surprisingly, the mood was still light and carefree. At this particular juncture, I was sitting in the middle portion of the boat. I didn't have access to my poncho at the time so I sat where there was a covering. Eventually, I had to put my poncho on because the rains started to get a bit ridiculous.

The rain just kept coming and coming. And coming. The posture of our trip went from light and carefree to concern. The expression of our driver said it all. We couldn't understand everything he was saying because of the language barrier but we *definitely* could understand his facial expressions. His gestures became more and more definitive as we navigated through rougher waters. Our boat driver was now standing in the back of the vessel making strong and precise directives. He started directing us to reposition ourselves to balance out the boat. This was the first sign of real trouble hitting the horizon.

I was one of the heavier people on the boat, so he told me and a few others to move up to the front to help balance us out, or so he had hoped. And then he told me to move up *way further*. I perched alongside two of the other leaders from the trip, Mike and Linda. They were at the very front of the boat. I was catty-cornered right behind them.

As I moved to the front I now had a very different perspective of what was going on. We were taking on a ton of water. This was an amount where more water was coming in then water going out. Visibility had started to become outrageous as well. From where I was positioned I could get a clear view of the back of the boat. As I looked I saw two of my teammates alongside our boat driver. There was a gap between us and them. I could see Adam and Courtney doing their best to bail out the water from the back of the boat. And our driver went from calm to frantic in a quick, but gradual motion. All of this happened in probably seconds but it felt like a longer time.

The driver was doing his best to steer but the wind and the waters would not cooperate. At this point we were way too far to go back the Mokan Island. And we were way too far from land to dock. We were literally in the middle of the Indian Ocean. At this point it became real! This is when you could see and feel a little bit of panic in the air. Not like 'screaming panic' but more like 'let's do what we can to live' kind of panic. We were now at the point where the boat could capsize. Officially we could now sink in the middle of nowhere.

This is where I remembered things starting to happen in a slow motion kind of way. I distinctly could remember the boat starting to sway out of control. Water was now lapping over the sides and into our vessel viscously. There was a span of time where we all were working together to prevent the boat from capsizing. There were a few us laid out, prostrate, trying to keep the boat from flipping over. We were doing our best to keep the boat steady. We made every effort to stay balanced.

It was so surreal. We vigorously tried to not flip, flop, or sink. And in the middle of it there were some strange moments of clarity. I remembered knowing in my head that the moment was dangerous but in my heart I was at peace. It felt like most of the people on our boat felt the same way too. I remembered saying to others and myself little words of encouragement and prayers. I remembered other people doing the same. There wasn't a real deathly panic like you would expect to happen at that time. You would think people would be looking towards a disastrous ending. Notably, the opposite occurred. There was a tangible peace intermingled in our time of turmoil.

I remembered distinctly thinking a few random things simultaneously. I remembered that the moment felt like something right out of the Bible. Something out of the Book of Mark or some gospel chapter. I also remembered thinking, I really hope everyone on this boat knows how to swim. Seriously. Later on I found out a few people didn't know how to swim. This blew my mind. Crazy!

Another thought that plagued my mind was sharks. Yes, sharks. I knew I could swim. I knew I didn't fit the stereotype of "black people and not swimming." I am no Michael Phelps but I can at least hold out for an adequate amount of time. I am pretty sure I could have made it to the shoreline from where we were, but I didn't want to test that theory *at all*. It was overcast and the visibility of the water was miserably low. Opaque couldn't describe it. I simply didn't want to swim and be caught by 'Jaws'. I know them sharks like dark meat.

I also remembered thinking, "God is with us." This thought went on and on for I don't know how long. I think I have a thing about repetition when something traumatic is occurring. Maybe it's a defense mechanism. The rains still kept coming. They were now hitting us at a sideways angle. It seemed like we were going to sink or do something unthinkable to survive or get out of the situation.

Fortunately, there was a break in the weather. I could have sworn I heard someone praying and in the midst of the prayers I could see the rains subside a little bit. I mean the rains definitely calmed down. And the best part was that we now could see land. The unfortunate part of this was that we still were too far from a legitimate port. We had nowhere to land. And the water had risen so much in our boat that we were about to lose power and control of our motor. This meant only one thing...

Before I tell you the end of the story, can you do me a favor? Please? Trying to capture the breadth and depth of our entire to trip to Thailand (and Cambodia) was difficult. After all, we did a little of everything on that trip. I couldn't see myself giving you every detail. I wanted to do that but it would be impossible. There were quite a few moments of seeking and finding God in both Thailand and Cambodia. So, I prayed. I asked God about which story or stories I should share with you at the moment. This story was the one that came to mind and heart.

I share this story to bring up something about God's nature. God is a good, good Father. He protects His children even when their natural fathers, mothers, and/or guardians cannot. Here's what we will do. Can you make me this promise? If we ever have the time and the chance, let me tell you the whole story of our trip. We can sit down, eat a meal and we can exchange life experiences. I can tell you the whole story then. And you can tell me some of your stories as well.

For now, let me center my focus in this way: In seeking and finding God, I have found that God is a great protector. He protected me then. He protected me on the bridge that one day. He will continue to protect you and me through all of our circumstances in a way He sees fit.

... We had to crash. It was our only viable option. We were taking in too much water. It was only a matter of time before we sunk. Our driver made the decision. It was final. We were going to find a patch of mangroves to crash into. Our motor was dancing on dangerous territory with the water that surrounded it. Adam and the boat driver were getting shocked but they didn't stop trying to keep the motor going. We had no dock or port in sight.

So it was. We headed straight for the mangroves. I think we had to come in at an angle. Either way, we came into the trees hot and heavy. Like the moment I had earlier, the impact had a slow motion feel to it. At the very front were Mike and Linda. Several people yelled duck. All you can hear were scrapings of trees. Branches were breaking left and right. Grumbles, groans, and grasping of solid objects followed. We braced ourselves for the worst. There was a slight hush and then a gasp. It was a gasp of relief. I don't how it happened but they were safe. We were all safe. Of all the trees in front of us, none of them impaled our leaders. In fact, no one on our boat was hurt at all. The trees had nestled us upon impact.

It was the perfect timing too. Minutes later out boat immediately starting sinking. Our items started floating all over the place. We quickly became the Swiss Family Robinsons. In a timely fashion, many of us took to the trees. This effort was mostly to salvage as many items as we could. You could just imagine all the items we had. We had smartphones galore that were drowning in salt water. Mine was in waterproof case. So, I was good in that regard. However, my wallet, unfortunately, was another thing. It went scuba diving in the ocean but it never came up for air.

Luckily, someone had a Thai phone in good working condition. With this we alerted the coast guards. Help was on the way. Although it felt like an eternity for them to come, they came and we were saved. It was insane that this happened to us, but what was more insane was our reaction to the situation. It was incredible. To this day I am still amazed of how joyful, grateful, and oddly happy we were as a group. In fact, our group had a pleasant reaction to the situation. We were singing and laughing all the way back to the mainland.

Honestly, it could only have been that particular group that would react the way we did. I believe this to be true because we all had a deep-seated belief in God that couldn't be shaken. We all shared a simplistic view about God. We believed God to be a good, faithful, and a great protector. He was a Father among fathers in that moment. He protected us in a very troubling time.

CHAPTER 6A

The Chair

There is chair in my room. It is the most comfortably uncomfortable chair I have ever sat in. Physically, it has a plush, inviting, soft wool-like interior. It boasts a concave vortex that calls you to sit down, relax, and forget your worries. I am convinced this little moon chair is one of the best inventions offered from the architectural and interior design worlds.

At the same time, I am conflicted in saying these words because it is such a painful chair to sit in as well. This same chair boasts an equally bold reputation of causing agony, uneasiness, and lots of tears. Sometimes the tears are joyful but oft times, not so joyful. It is a painful chair because it is where God has chosen to speak to me about my wounds and scars from the past and present.

It is also a place where honesty reigns. Conversations from the heart occur there. The passions, the worries, and the joys of the heart are expressed in unapologetic form on the chair. From this place the thoughts of my mind are released. When I sit in this chair, being silent, I can actually feel the honest truth. I sit on that piece of furniture and I face the unblemished reality of life. The experience sometimes makes me squirm, but this is the place where God deals with my heart.

The whole idea of the chair came from a counselor I consistently met with for about a year. During a session, he challenged me to find a regular spot to meet with God in my house. He suggested that I purchase a chair to sit in to do the processing of my memories. This experience can be tortuous I tell you. But it also has the capacity of pleasantness too.

The chair idea comes from a biblical text in Lamentations. Lamentations 3:25-29:

> *"The Lord is good to those who wait for him, to the soul who seeks him. It is good that one should wait quietly for the salvation of the Lord. It is good for a man that he bears the yoke in his youth. Let him sit alone in silence when it is laid on him; let him put his mouth in the dust— there may yet be hope..."*

The chair embraces the aforementioned scripture. It encapsulates the whole idea of dealing with your junk (one's issues) while one is young. It is to sit still. It is to face the pain lodged within. It is to grovel in the dust and the rocky situations life has dealt you and me. It is to place our hope in a Father who will be our salvation in the midst of our distress ...

I am really debating whether or not to be vulnerable in this moment. Or at least, I am trying to figure out, how I should proceed in my sharing. Here is what I am thinking: *Why should I be naked when you are sitting, reading this book with your clothes on? This situation makes me feel vulnerable and that sounds like a bad deal to me.*

The only things that keep me going forward in sharing these thoughts with you are: my purpose, my trust in my Heavenly Father, and the hope that my sharing will be helpful. Hopefully,

I will help someone, other than myself, in a significant way. Hopefully, that person I am being vulnerable for is you.

Remember when I told you about the time I was in silence? The week of silence? Well, one of my goals in silence and solitude was to gain a better understanding of my purpose and become settled in who I am.

The best two metaphors that describe who I am are an "usher" and a "bridge." An usher, because I love bringing people into the presence of God. My friend Pete Jenkins coined that phrase. My life is meant to point people in the direction of where God is and to remind my community that He is still here with us. He is still engaged with His creation.

I am also meant to be a bridge. A bridge that connects people. More specifically, I am meant to connect people who otherwise would not be connected. I am meant to bring worlds of great difference into the unity of Christ. I am conduit of connection in between the chasms that separate the marginalized, minority, and the majority of various cultures.

To do such things means that I have to lose something of myself in the process. I have to be willing to lose my life. To lose "me." After all, there is no greater gift than losing one's life for friends. And one way to do that is to share my story. Consequently, my friends, I will share this part of my story. The story from the chair.

Currently, I am dealing with three things. They are the three topics that my chair time has been focused on. They are: Intimacy, loneliness, and my struggle of loving Jesus, but dealing with the inner conflict of same sex attractions.

In my early days of my chair time I would center my processing of thoughts with a prompt. Typically, it would be a question my counselor Ryan would give me to answer. I would spend my time alone processing a wound or a memory and it would be centered on a theme. Later on I would share my thoughts of this time in a counseling session.

Two questions that stood out to me quite clearly in the beginning of my chair times were these: *What are you grieving? And what are the real longings you seek that may be experienced in different ways?* These questions are enveloped in layers. And these questions, more often than not, are connected to two common themes of my grief.

The typical themes that these questions brought about were on the topics of loneliness and intimacy. More succinctly, loneliness and the fear of not being able to achieve intimacy in long term relationships. Or even achieving intimacy with people period. Whether it is friendships, community, or with family.

The ultimate experience in seeking God is finding something in Him that we cannot find in any other person, place, or thing in the world. It's the thing that you and I have wanted the most in our lives. It is intimacy. It is love in its purest, revealed form. In particular, it is being known as we are and being loved just the way we are. Although not staying in the same position of where we are. It is finding enjoyment in one another and vice versa. It is laying our lives down for the utter joy given to another person. It is dying so that the other person can live. It is choosing others first. It's that thing inside of us that cries out for closeness with God and with others.

Intimacy is a tricky thing for me. I desperately want to experience it but I find myself turned into a pile of ash every time I truly try to get close or go deeper in relationships. I view intimacy as a fire I am drawn to but it is a flame that hurts me every time I get *too* close.

Intimacy, thus far in my life, has been an unquenchable fire that I cannot bear. The thought of my attempts to be intimate with God and people depresses me to no end. Thus far, I cannot solve it. The conundrum is that I love it, possess it, fight it, and push it away all at the same time. It is a frustrating thing, seeing that I am a follower of Jesus. Somehow, I have figured that by now I would be a better recipient and giver of love and intimacy. I am woefully far from where *I think I ought* to be.

With God I try to get close and I achieve some ground for weeks. Sometimes months and years, but inevitably I turn to the most putrid of vices to escape the intensity. I don't know if other people have experienced this but when I truly get close to God it is astounding. It is unparalleled and remarkable. Nevertheless, it is simultaneously the most uncomfortable thing to experience. (This experience is also mirrored in relationships with people. Especially in my attempts at romantic relationships with women.)

The intensity with God is a whole world in itself. I have found out that God has layers. He has depth. He has a holiness that I can't quite describe. He possesses an otherworldliness that my spirit knows. It is kindred to me but my body can't seem to contain the magnitude.

I got to be honest. Often times my more intimate moments with God are followed by pain, frustration, sin, and depression. Sometimes it is so bad that I go numb for weeks. I have complained to God about it. It scares me and frustrates me that I am unable to remain in God's presence consistently and the way I would like.

Pornography is the worst for me because it is probably the greatest antithesis of intimacy ever created. Unfortunately, there have been several cycles of great intensity and intimacy with God after which I have ended up on pornography binges, relapses, and depression. All of these have been my choices; that is my ugly truth.

Intimacy, unmet and/or inappropriately satisfied, can lead us into all sorts of unsightly paths. When you are starving for intimacy, your souls screams in agony. And if this appetite goes unchecked, it can lead you to find love in all the wrong places. At least that's what my experience has taught me. I have also found that intimacy is a profound mechanism in which God directs us to Himself. For me, I have found that the tenderness and companionship of God is only a few drops of tears, or an authentic prayer away, when I am yearning for intimacy. Many times in my frail search for intimacy, I have ran into a Father who has been patiently waiting for me to stop, be still, and let Him love me. And I to love Him.

In grad school I had a relationship that most people didn't know about. It was a relationship that went undefined for weeks. Infatuation and the fancied thoughts of being liked, and liking someone else, abounded in our connection, but nothing ever amounted in a long-term relationship. The relationship had all types of red flags that spoke codependency all over it. Sadly, at the time I didn't understand such terminology. I just knew that we were kind of having a good time just being with each other. Kind of.

Truth be told, I was uneasy the whole time that we were together. However, I had no real balls in that relationship. I just kept going along with the ride, while all the time I just wanted to simply have a friendship. Kind of. Ugh. And she was aggressive. She definitely was wearing the pants in our relationship, so to speak.

It's the worse feeling in the world when you feel like you are settling. I knew we were not going to be good for each other in the long run but I was so lonely. At the time, the mutuality of being wanted and cared for was an electricity I was willing to be shocked by. On paper, we were sort of a good match for each other. Life experience and vocational direction seemed to be lining up but God already warned me. He had made it known to me earlier on that we were going to hurt each other if we stayed together. I dragged my feet in all of this. I did not speak up in setting healthy boundaries. Neither of us did. This only could end in flames.

There was one evening when we were hanging out together. We were supposed to be working on assignments for class. Homework was to be our focus. Unbeknownst to me, she had other ideas. She started kissing up on my neck. Most would see this as a straightforward sexual gesture. This moment triggered something in me. However, it wasn't something erotic. To her, and my surprise, I didn't reciprocate in her advances. I just sort of sat there frozen.

She then told me some words that further paralyzed me. She mentioned something on the lines of me not reciprocating. And it made her concerned as to whether our relationship was going to last. Every word that she said brought me to a place of shame. All I heard were haunting words and phrases. You are not good enough. You are not man enough. You will never have a wife. You will always be lonely.

The words and negativity just kept flooding. I can't remember her actually saying those words, but I heard them nonetheless. They most likely came from the enemy of my soul. I don't think she meant for that particular effect, but it just kept coming like fiery darts.

Somehow, I had moved from her room to the living room. In the living room I ended up sitting in a creaky wooden chair. It was not a pleasant piece of furniture to sit on. Mostly because I wanted to run out of the house but I couldn't move. While sitting there, I had an outer body experience. Eerie wasn't even the first words to describe it. I remembered seeing myself outside of myself. (I have come to learn that this manifestation has happened to other people who have gone through significant trauma- especially involving physical and sexual abuse. This was my case).

In the image I was floating above myself and looking down at a version of me sitting in the chair. Inside of me and sitting in the chair there was a little boy. The boy kept saying, "I feel like a little kid, I feel like a little kid." Hello! I thought. You are a little boy! The problem is that you are trapped in a grown man's body.

I couldn't stop saying it. I can't even remember when I finally left her house. It felt like hours, like a really long day that wouldn't end, but somehow it ended. Consequently, for months I went into a stupor. Depression was the bread that I ate every day. I tried to end our relationship. And then I tried to just be friends. I could tell she would never have been satisfied with just being friends. So, I finally came to my senses and listened to my Father and the godly counsel of friends and family. I couldn't be around her. I ended all contact with her.

I ended that relationship and began dealing with some serious wounds in my soul. It marked the beginning of seeking help. I began seeking for help because I knew something had seriously gone wrong in my heart. It had to deal with issues of the past. There were arrows in my soul that needed plucking. I had an intimacy issue.

The catalyst of pushing my healing process forward came from a teaching assistant named Kimberly. In a passing conversation she noted something that took me by surprise. I was trying to impress her with how well I was balancing the challenges I had in my life. I told her of all the activities I was in, the jobs I were holding, the class load I was enduring, and the sport teams I was excelling in and on.

She was unimpressed. Without skipping a beat she made a remark that floored me. She looked at me with sincerity. She said, "With all the activities that you are doing, doesn't it seem like you are running away from something?" I was caught off guard. It was shocking to have someone see right through me. She saw me beyond my masquerades and attempts "to keep it all together."

What could I say? She was right. Spot on. And with that I began dealing with my junk for real. I began to be proactive in my healing process. It was the spark I needed to face the truth. I had an intimacy issue. Now, before you get your hopes up. I don't want you think that this going to be some fantastic testimony of healing. Because I don't have that kind of story- yet.

What do I have is this. I do have a story of God being Immanuel in my brokenness. Immanuel means 'God with us'. That's who God has been to me. He has been with me when I have needed, wanted, and desired intimacy, love, and the intangibles that this world can't even begin to provide.

In that time I also began to sense God in a place that I never realized He had been. God is the one person who has always been with me in my loneliness. Even when I didn't know it, He was there. He has repeatedly been in the place where I have hidden, felt forgotten, or unknowingly fell in.

Loneliness is an interesting place to be found in. And I think it is a highly unique place that seems to be unique to each person.

Everyone has their own story with loneliness. Yet, loneliness is completely common. Actually, it is dreadfully common and basic. Every person has faced it at some point or another in their life. And even if it goes by a different face- it is still the same.

The trick that the enemy of our soul wants us to believe is that our personal loneliness is so unique to us that no one, not even God, can understand us. This lie is meant to have us believe that we are so weird and so different from others that we are beyond the capability of being helped or loved.

That is exactly how I felt about the loneliness attached to my same sex attractions. Many times I felt as though my struggle was the most unique and complex struggle. Unknowingly, I built walls all around my heart because I thought my struggle was so different from any other person. I became fearful that people, even my own family, would not love me if they knew what I struggled with.

It was when I started seeking help, asking hard questions, and sharing my story that I began to see the truth. And it was when I started going to Living Waters that I began finding peace in my places of loneliness and frustration. Sitting here in my chair, I can remember it and see it so clearly...

CHAPTER 6B

The Chair

... After my encounter with Kimberly I was convinced that I needed help. I couldn't pinpoint all of it, but I knew something was majorly wrong deep down inside. Her direct words made sense to me. They hit me hard. They came in like a wrecking ball. All of a sudden, I could see my issues plainly. I couldn't deny it. My life was in shambles on the inside. Metaphorically speaking, the face of my house looked great, but my interior structures were dilapidating rapidly. I was a house of cards ready to fall at the slightest of breezes.

See that's the thing with me. I have always been the type of person who was constantly "happy" on the exterior. On the outside I always carried the facade of being a nice person who continually had it together. My outside didn't always match with my inside. Many of us struggle with that, eh?

Now, most of it wasn't fake, but sometimes I would still be happy outwardly when inside I was dying. Those of you with a similar disposition know that this is a great way to defend yourself from pain. The truth of the matter was this: I was sincerely a joyful person **but** I also carried some significant wounds in my heart.

These were wounds I had never dealt with. However, at that point in my life, I had to admit them. I was a depressed person fighting to live joyfully. And I could equally say that I was a joyful person fighting depression. Sometimes the blurred lines of my polarity caused me fits of frustration inside and out.

When I had that aforementioned outer body experience, I came face to face with the ugly in me. I noticed that I was actually in a continued cycle of depression, recovery, ascension, mountain top moments, joy, trauma, tripping, crashing, and falling back into the valley of depression again. Rinse and repeat: that was my life.

At that time in my life I went through a three month period where I would sleep for at least 12 hours a day. I would only get up to go to the most poignant grad school classes. I would only eat food if it was necessary. Day after day I would wade through a pile of trash and unsightly laundry in order to get out of my room.

I wouldn't see sunlight most days. It was as if I possessed a vampire complex. I would block calls from friends and family. And at that particular point in life, I never had the energy to fake it like I was doing great. I just simply shut people out because being "happy" was draining. I would say no to invitations, even though I desperately wanted to be with people. I would play volleyball everyone once in a while as an escape and coping mechanism. I thought the light-hearted setting of volleyball was a place that I could at least hide in the crowd and make a few people laugh. And then there was pornography, overeating, and the cave. It was all too much. It was all too overwhelming. I needed help and there were only two things stopping me from getting it - my pride and my shame.

I don't know why but I have always had an issue with my pride. I don't have that arrogant, in your face type of pride. I have more of a false humility, quietly patting myself on the back, self-righteous, judgmental, and perfectionist kind of pride. It's the type you can't always see right away but most definitely can feel it, if you are sensitive to that kind of thing.

I also have the "I can do it all by myself" and "look what I can do on my own" type of pride. This is the type where people like myself take great honor in being self-made and achieving feats by our own merit. This in reality is not a very godly quality to possess but it is something I do quietly struggle with. The funny thing is that you may never assume or presume it of me.

The origin of my pride maybe a result of learning to do a lot of things on my own as a kid. Or it might have to do with the fact that I grew up with my Jamaican immigrant grandparents. There are somethings you have to learn to do on your own when you have a generational and cultural gap. Hence, when push comes to shove I have often felt more comfortable getting jobs done on my own, especially if my teammates are not self-motivated or team-oriented.

Why do I do this? Well, I don't want to let anyone down. And let's face it, I don't want to let myself down either. Internally, I've seen it this way: If the ball is in my court than I am the only one to blame. I am the only one responsible. And it often felt better if I knew I was the only person I would hurt. As a result this would also help me avoid being hurt by others as well.

And there was also the trust factor. I think my pride might also have to do with a lack of trust. I have trust issues, y'all. I don't know why I just went into a Southern accent in that moment, but seriously, I have had to wrestle to let go a lot of things in my life. I'm sure you can understand.

The other yin to this yang is shame. Boy, I can't stand shame. I think this might be the worst feeling ever to be cast upon the soul of humanity. It can't be denied. Shame is definitely a direct result of sin. I hate the feeling of shame. Mostly because it paralyzes me in the most significant areas of my life.

To be honest, this book might have another, alternate purpose. I think I kind of wrote this book because I am tired of feeling shame. Especially, the shame of things done to me and the things I have done that I am not proud to admit. Shame has the ability to be a destiny killer. And for me, it was the thing that kept me from speaking up and being bold. It was the one weapon that shot me in the foot anytime I felt I was supposed to be confident in Christ.

I have had shame for all kinds of things. Some are major and some are minor. I have had shame over the most annoying things too. For example, I have felt shame in my younger years about the way my voice sounded. It's something about the octave of my voice. The timbre of my speaking voice lives in awkward range. It's not quite high enough but also not quite low enough.

My shame didn't stop there though. I have had shame for my body image at times. I have had shame for struggling with same sex attractions. I have had shame for being "an overly emotional kid" who could cry at the drop of a hat. In middle school, I have had shame for wearing "Bobos." Bobos are shoes that are non-name brand- if you didn't know. If you lived in an urban setting, you couldn't be caught dead (or alive) wearing them without dealing with middle school consequences.

And I have even had shame over the vehicle that my grandfather drove in my adolescence. It was an old beater of a vehicle that had holes in it. Literally, it had holes in it. It was the type of van that rained on the inside and outside when storms came through our Florida summers.

I say all of this not just for my own benefit. I say it for your benefit as well. If you are seeking God and you are also seeking freedom, than listen to this. **You have to lose your pride and your shame** if you want grow in intimacy with God and others. That's what I have learned.

I carried all of these multilayered intricacies and wounds within me for years. I lived with unresolved hate and anger for years. However, it wasn't until I went to Living Waters that I dealt head-on with my wounds, my pride, and my shame. It was a timely encounter that met me when I needed it the most.

Living Waters was a 5 month program for people experiencing relational and sexual brokenness. It was a space of healing for people dealing with wounds, abuse, and/or trauma. It was a place for people who had hang-ups and habits that were taking over their lives. It was a sanctuary for people who loved Jesus but had trouble getting over their addictions and ill-fated memories.

I found myself amidst this community in January 2010. I initially came for shallow reasons to be quite honest. My reasons for going to Living Waters were mainly to get rid of my pornography addiction and hopefully get 'fixed' emotionally and relationally. At the time, my end goal was to lose all of my bad habits and 'fix' my sexuality. In the end my hope was to become whole enough that I could get married to a wonderful woman of God, have a family, and become a "normal" person obtaining the "typical" Evangelical American Dream. And consequently, I would fill that intimacy hole dwelling in my heart. Then, and only then, I would live happily ever after with the companion of my dreams and my children at my side.

Needless to say, that is not what happened. What happened to me in Living Waters was much better and long-lasting. For starters, I gained a richness in love. I have learned to communicate better with people. I have learned to trust more and become vulnerable in appropriate ways. I have gained a better sense of boundaries and I have learned to protect and share my heart in more balanced, God honoring, and meaningful ways.

A lot happened to me and my fellow community in that time. We met every Tuesday for 5 months in a row. Every meeting brought me closer to my truest heart's desires and I began to experience intimacy like hadn't before. Not only me, but my fellow compatriots as well.

Like I said, Living Waters didn't answer my prayers like I thought it could or would. I am not married. I am 33 year old virgin, who, to be real, is still looking and longing for authentic companionship. I still have a desire to be with a woman whom God grants me a reciprocal love relationship. I'm indeed still desirous of my dance partner, but I am not stuck there. Marriage is not my end goal. And my life is not on hold until I have a wife and kids. Although deep down in my soul I believe I will have this great treasure one day, I have nonetheless, become better at enjoying what is occurring in the now. Living Waters gave me a better perspective of living life in the present.

Living Waters in many ways brought me back to the Garden of Eden. It brought me back to my truest and first love. It brought me back into honest dialogue with my Creator. Who knew that God could be so empathetic and so understanding of all the complexities that make up our lives- and my life in particular?

What was so helpful with Living Waters was that its focus wasn't on healing a particular wound or addiction. I loved the fact that Living Waters didn't make its focus on "fixing our issues." The focus was on connecting with Jesus. Consequently, healing occurred as a byproduct. This healing happened in varying degrees.

Something I realized in my time of Living Waters was that I idolized marriage more than I desired to be in a marriage. Marriage in my eyes equaled success. In fact, marriage was a type of telos to me. It was an arrival point- the pinnacle of success. Up to that point, I have seen it as a mile marker- the zenith of achievement. It was the one Boy Scout merit badge that I had never received. It was the one fish I have never been able to catch. I was unnecessarily unhappy because I hadn't achieved this unspoken goal.

Besides this, I learned other things in Living Waters as well. LW taught me to be relational again. It taught me to deal with my bitterness. I had so much hate in my heart towards my family and others who have mistreated me or misunderstood me. And I was so hurt by things I didn't understand and things that no one would dare to address. I had father wounds, mother wounds, trust issues, and disappoints for legitimate and illegitimate reasons.

One of most profound experiences that happened at LW was learning the practices of confession and honest prayer. These were the disciplines that my soul craved and I didn't know it but once I practiced them I instantly connected to God in an unexpected way.

Clarifications are due to you as a reader. When I say confession, I don't mean meeting a man or woman in a booth or seeing a priest to pour out my dark confessions in anonymity. Although this could be quite helpful in the right context. What I am talking about is speaking to God plainly and freely without pretenses, ornate speech, or falsehoods. In other words it's naked talk. It is speaking honestly to God from the heart.

In addition, when I say confession I also don't mean listing out all my sins to ask God, or a person, for penance or forgiveness. Confession, as I learned from LW, is just simply being honest about everything with God. It is confessing the state of your weakness, confessing your love for God, confessing one's present state of affairs as it is. It is admitting where you are in life in order to be completely honest with God. And subsequently, doing the same with people.

I learned about confession by somewhat of a dramatic means. A wonderful aspect of LW is that the program utilizes a lot of experiential activities to engage the group and individuals in connecting with God and each other.

One day we had this activity of prayer and confession at the foot of a cross. A large cross was brought into our meeting room. It had the trappings and feel of an authentic cross; it had a New Testament appeal to it. One that transported my community and myself into a place of authenticity.

What taught me true confession was hearing the authentic prayers of our community. People were not praying to be heard by others. They were praying because their hearts were unbearably full. And they needed to pour this fullness on to the feet of Jesus in that time. They did it right there at the foot of the cross. The prayers, especially of one of my friends, brought me to place of vulnerability. In that place I found God to be nearer than ever. And it actually has become a constant theme of my life. I have become a person of honest prayer and confession.

Confession and honest prayer, especially in my chair, have been my steady diet of seeking and finding God. I found God to be the nearest to me, and I to Him, when I am humble, humbled, and humiliated. I have found that when you pray honestly to God, He is often to be found very close. It is as though our sincere words from our hearts woo Him. Such words, with untainted and sincere meaning, are a perfumes released from our soul. God is attracted to that sort of thing.

Now, confession and honest prayer are great, but they need to be coupled with community. Life does not happen in a vacuum or on an island. And true freedom is likewise. Being at LW was incredible because of the community. It was really helpful for me to be in community during that time of my life. It's hard not to state the obvious but it is true. You can't live on confession and prayer alone. You have to live life with others.

Prior to LW, what often hindered me in community was perfection. My church upbringing, cultural upbringing, and societal upbringing taught me to hide imperfections and to appear fine all the time. And I believed I had to do that until I couldn't do it anymore.

I wanted real love and real relationships. And what I have found is that real love and real relationships encounter messiness. This is the sort of thing I had craved in deepest part of my heart. I wanted to be around a community of people who were completely themselves. I wanted to be around people who could reciprocally love me even though I was a mess. That is something seldom found in our society, cultures, and churches. But that is something I found in LW. And once you have experienced that it is hard to go back.

It's not about living in a place of constant pain or reliving bad memories. It is about living with honesty and support. It was about having a community of people who can deal with that fact that we aren't perfect people, but we are willing to grow better day by day and help each other in our shortcomings. It is to have Jesus be our head and we be His body. It is to function with each other as one. It is to help other parts of the body in times of need. It is to function with each other in harmony. I loved Living Waters because of these things. I sought and found God in this place.

Speaking of community, I think it is time for me to get out of this chair. I want tell you about another type of community. It is one near and dear to my heart. It is one of my favorite communities of all times. It is a community found in Purdy, Missouri. It is a camp called ...

CHAPTER 7

Camp Barnabas

What a place! It wrecked my life in a good way. I am indebted to the wonderful 140 acres of land found in Purdy, Missouri. I spent four summers during college and 2 years of my post-graduate life there. I am highly grateful for this little nook in the world.

On the surface, it was a summer camp for kids and adults with various types of abilities and disabilities. It was a camp that ran for nine weeks. In those nine weeks, kids and adults from all over the Midwest, The South, and other regions in the United States came to spend an unforgettable week at camp. It was a week where people, who most often have been defined solely by their disabilities, could enjoy a portion of life beyond the labels. They could immerse themselves in fun, adventure, Jesus' love, and embrace the phrase "I can."

When I say campers embraced the phrase "I can!" I mean this with no exaggeration. I have seen campers who are blind have the opportunity to shoot rifles- with great accuracy I might add. I have seen campers who have immobility in their limbs cruise through a ropes course, with the aid of our ropes facilitation team. Mind you, this is a ropes course suspended between 45 to 60 feet in the air with various challenging elements.

I have gone spelunking, cave exploring, with campers who wanted to beat their fear of the dark while traveling in tight, narrow spaces. I have gone camping in the woods with friends who did not let their disabilities dictate whether they can do survival training. I have flown in a plane with a camper with autism who had a mild fear of heights but still chose to challenge himself. In short, almost all things are made possible at camp!

Below the surface there is another layer to camp. It is powerful. In that layer there is something supernatural happening. It's a place where love abounds, along with patience, joy, frustration, peace and agony. A plethora of emotions and actions live in harmony on those hallowed grounds in Missouri. Life fully expressed occurs intensely at Camp Barnabas. I have wept a lot and I have marveled aplenty at young men and women who have shown me a thing or two about life. This place seemed to bring out the best (and sometimes the worst) in every person that sets afoot there. It's not only the campers that were amazing but it's the volunteers and staff too.

Imagine if you will, a place where everyone is determined to serve each other before they serve themselves. A place where people are determined to make each week the best week ever for all campers, volunteers, and staff alike. A place like heaven but on earth. I really can't think of place like it. To this day I still can't replace it in my life. It's a community like no other. Words that I speak about it cannot do it justice.

Every person who has been there will say the same thing I am going to say. You have to participate in camp to really understand it. You have to visit camp to know the beauty, the magic, and the uniqueness it possesses. If it were not for this place, I sincerely would not understand the ways of Jesus as I do now. I would be devoid of understanding humanity as it should and could be. Concepts such as humility, serving others, dying to self, loving for the sake of love, would be foreign to me. This place was, and is, life-changing for all that have entered. I am included in that number...

It was the first summer of my freshman year at college. I was in a group called FX. We were on tour, travelling to twelve states in a couple of broke down vehicles. That was a story unto itself. FX, was a percussion performance group from my university. We were similar to STOMP or a Blue Man group. We did performances, shared the love of Jesus, and motivated people through percussion, dance, rhythm, and words of inspiration.

Our group was in the middle of our summer tour when I needed to do a Staff Training Week at camp. My connecting route to camp was to take a bus from Kentucky to Missouri. And when I was done with Staff Week, I would meet up with the FX group in North Carolina. Like always, I love to travel on a color-filled and outlandish path. My first journey to Barnabas was without exception. It was "interesting" and adventurous. Let's be honest, I seldom travel an uneventful route. It's rare for me to have a straight forward journey.

I would get to camp by Greyhound which means I was subjecting myself to a soap opera on wheels. I took a 26 hour trip from Bowling Green, Kentucky to Springfield, Missouri on the way up to camp. And on the way back I took a 32 hour trip from Springfield, MO to somewhere I can't remember in North Carolina. A lot happened in that time. For one, I lost my ticket on the journey. That could have ended my trip quickly. I really didn't have the money to buy a new ticket. Thankfully the lady at the register was kind enough to issue me a new ticket. She could tell it was my first time traveling like this.

Now, what happened on the Greyhound needs to stay on the Greyhound. But what I can say, I will say. In short, the bus driver got pulled over for reckless driving, I heard the most vilest of comments between strangers, saw the most obscene sites between friends of promiscuity, and I also met an evangelist who might have been an angel in disguise. He shared the gospel with me in Spanglish. Let's just say that by the time we were done with the bus ride, I couldn't wait to arrive to Camp Barnabas.

Keep this in mind, I only knew of this place by internet and phone. I had never been to camp physically. All prior communication was done at a long distance. My interview and hiring process were a couple of phone calls and faxes. I only knew the voices of the Camp Directors, some staff, and other camp personnel. So, everything about camp was going to be foreign to me. I did not know how far in the boondocks it would be. I wasn't sure if there would be some bears in dem woods. In fact, it was first time to be in a wooded area for an extended period of time. So naturally I could hear the music. (Cue scary backwoods music.) Just kidding.

Something else to note, I was never meant to work at this place. I was actually applying for another camp that works with kids in the inner city. The short story is that they didn't have enough spots for the particular job I wanted to do but they liked me. I guess I impressed with my interview. Consequently, they referred me to several camps in the area. Camp Barnabas was one of them. I say this because I felt out of place when I first got to camp. A bit awkward is the word. I was planning to work at a nearby camp that would have felt a little more comfortable to me. However, I ended up in a place that would stretch me in that very same comfort.

The awkwardness started when I got to the bus depot in Springfield, MO. I got there and waited for an hour. My phone was dead and I didn't think to have a sign that said "Hi, I am Gary Francis the only brown-skinned man in this bus depot."

Funny thing is the person picking me up had a hard time finding me. This could have been avoided. No one told her that I was Jamerican. I figured that would have helped. Haha!!!

When we got to camp it was midnight. People we already settled in. In fact, most were dead asleep. The awkwardness continued as I fumbled my way to bed in the dark. It was the first time that I was to sleep in an oversized tent called a yurt. The awkwardness didn't end there. In the morning I learned quickly about camp culture. The first introduction was a bit of a rude awakening. I was literally blown away. Or, to be more specific, blown awake.

One of the traditions of camp was to do interesting and outlandish "wake-up" times. My first morning at camp started with a leaf blower shocking me out of sleep. Some guy I didn't know opened the door and set my ears on fire with the chainsaw sounds of a leaf-blower. I can't remember if I found that moment to be amusing at the time, but I do remember thinking this place was definitely different from what I was used to. I also remembered seeing the reactions of the other staff members. They seemed not too surprised by it. It was as though this was a mild and amusing wake up to them. They gave an air of normalcy to the event. After this, we had approximately 30 minutes to get ready. I met a few people and did light introductions in between brushing teeth, showering, making up my bed, and tucking my sleeping bag away. We then made our way down to IP. IP is short for Inspiration Point.

Inspiration Point is set atop of a bluff. The scenery there was breathtaking. The view always seemed to be attractive. In the distance you would see nothing but rolling hills, beautiful greenery, and the intricacies of farm living. Below the horizon line you could see and hear the trickling and rushing water of a creek that rested 60 feet below. For a nature lover like me, it was quite a sight to behold. In the future, I would come to find

Inspiration Point's beauty several times a day. I would visit early in the morning, at sunset, during the night with the fireflies, or when a storm was about to roll in. During that specific morning, however, the beauty was a minor feature in the background.

At IP we typically started our time by singing silly songs and doing ridiculous chants. All of this was foreign to me, but I can't lie, I found it undeniably hilarious and welcoming. Especially, because every person was incredibly invested in the chants and cheers. These were college-aged students yelling at the top of their lungs. They uttered the silliest phrases and songs. *Grey Squirrel, Little Cabin in the Woods, Heart-Shaped Box* were to name a few. The songs were all sung with enthusiasm and vigor.

In all of this I found myself confused, yet I totally joined in the madness. Even though campers were not present, the level of excitement was ultra-high. Again, you have to be at camp to *really* understand it. Right after chants and cheers there was an IP speaker. This is a person who comes up and speaks on a scripture, a theme, and/or inspirational words. It can oftentimes be a really empowering moment. It's a great way to start off the day.

Before the IP speaker spoke there was a lull moment. It was a small enough lull for me to realize something. I tried not to let it get to me but I sat in the crowd and recognized it. I was the only dark brown man in the crowd. In fact I was the only person who was "black" on staff. This had its advantages and disadvantages. I would learn of this throughout the years. It felt awkward at the time but I just let the moment pass on so I can enjoy my new surroundings. I didn't want to dwell on it too much. At least not then. There were too many new things going on in my system to process it. So, I simply listened to the prayers. I listened to the speaker. And I embraced the awkwardness of it all.

That week at camp didn't follow the typical pattern of a regular summer camp week because it was a training week. Our time was different and our focus was different too but the heart of camp was more than alive and very much the same when it came to camp culture. Our sole focus was on three things that week. They were on work projects, being trained for our experience with campers and volunteers, and bonding with our staff team and God. Each element was necessary and well-received.

Work projects were surprisingly one of the most enjoyable moments of camp. Not necessarily because of the tasks themselves. Although, I must admit, digging post holes, building fences from scratch, and using hammers for necessary and unnecessary means was fun. However, it was the bonding and unity that I loved the most. This type of connection was the spark that got our communal engine going.

Up to that point in my life, I had never really met such a unique group of individuals. I mean, a group who relished doing work together. It truly inspired me. The bigger the project, the greater the joy we would have. After a few tasks, I started anticipating the joy we would have once we finished a humongous task together. It was great.

When we weren't doing work projects we were in training. This consisted of countless things. We did CPR and FIRST AID training. We learned about assisting individuals with everyday activities of daily living. We learned what to do when someone is having a seizure. We learned about the differences between cystic fibrosis, hemophilia, neurofibromatosis, lymphoma, and ataxia telclasia. We learned a lot! Undoubtedly though, the most powerful thing I learned in Staff Week was something small and simple. It was so simple that it really changed the course of my life. My whole entire outlook on interacting with people changed because of it.

We learned about People First Language and Person First thinking. The concept was oh so simplistic but yet so profound. The whole idea behind people first language is seeing people as *who* they are before *what* label they might be connected to. It is to see the person first, before an attribute or an adjective that is linked to them. I can hear it clearly in my mind. I can hear Cindy Teas explain it. She said it in her Texan drawl, "instead of saying that autistic boy, you should say that boy with Autism." A person is more valuable than a physical trait or condition. She would add something to this affect, "How would you like to be known by something trivial rather than something from your character -you being you?"

Person first is a concept not solely based on words but on the heart. To me I took the idea as a challenge for life. It was a concept that transcended not only the world of people experiencing disability-but all spheres of life. It was a concept that stood in stark opposition to our society at large. In the US, we are notorious for living in opposition to this concept. We typically address people primarily by some outward characteristic that is grouped into commonly used labels. We use terms such as the "black guy," "the chubby girl over there," "the cross eyed one," and so on and so forth as our means to identify people. Rarely do we describe the character of a person first. Nor do we seek it first. (I digress. I digress and I will say this. That small concept took ahold of me right away. As soon as camp started I saw people in a different light.)

There was one camper in particular that helped me understand the beauty of person first thinking. He was a person who helped me to understand God in way I had never done before. His name was Judd. In him I found a fountain called love and life. I found God in him. Judd had a smile and gentle way about him that drew you into mystery. His eyes spoke love and invitation.

He knew how to pierce the heart in a good way. And he knew how to silence the masses.

Judd. Just saying his name makes me smile. Now, here's the thing. I really can't explain myself completely when it comes to Judd because most of my relationship with him was unspoken. Literally unspoken. Like I said before, our relationship wasn't based on words. In fact, Judd had Angelman's Syndrome, a complex genetic disorder that primarily affects the nervous system. Some of the features of this condition include delayed development, intellectual disability, severe speech impairment, and problems with movement and balance. Judd had all of the mentioned characteristics, nevertheless, he spoke to me in volumes.

To love and know Judd, I had to do something I didn't know how to do. It was something he taught me. I had to learn to love somebody on their terms- not mine. As much as I was a "loving person" at the time, the truth would reveal that I had a harder time loving people then I previously believed. It was foreign to me. The world of Judd. His world constantly left me speechless. How do you love someone without words? How do you communicate without mutual verbal dialogue?

Yet he drew me into something I hadn't known before; a selflessness slowly began to develop in me. The only way I could truly understand Judd was to suspend my needs and wants in exchange for his. My heart became clay in relating to him. More than anyone I had known, Judd taught me the ways of true love. Love that is directed by small continuous choices done in long periods of time. This is contrary to the prevailing false sense of love which is all about temporary feelings.

Again, it is hard to explain, but he taught me how to do simple things well. Listening beyond the ears was his key way to teach me. Never have I listened so intently. I listened because I wanted to know how to love him well. Everyday tasks were slowed down when he was around, but I really enjoyed it. My senses were disciplined around Judd. My voice and depth in delivery were hushed to a loud whisper. My thoughts were centered. My hands and feet became more other-focused and other-centered. My limbs became bereft of wantonness. My sense of smell was even tweaked a little bit too.

At one point I remembered having this peculiar feeling that we both had come to a place where we could read each other's minds. Not in a creepy way but in an "I understand you bro" without words kind of way. But it was his laughter that really made me know we were connected. His laugh was guttural and authentic. Life with Judd was more about rhythm rather than pace. Communication with him was clear when the silent tempo of mutual care and concern were at a simple and harmonious beat. Humanity made more sense around him. I know this all sounds a bit mystical and bit enigmatic but this is the best way I can describe my interactions with Judd.

I found a bit of the Father hidden inside of Judd and in Camp Barnabas in general. And I somehow want to relay this truth about men and women like Judd. People whom we label, that have disabilities, are people who often carry keys of life, love, and lessons we all can appreciate in this world. We have to see people first before their exterior in order for all people to come alive. We need this perspective to understand Love better. We need this in order for God to be known as He is. We need to this perspective in order to survive.

Now don't get me wrong, Judd also knew how to push my buttons. He is the type of person that could keep you up at night by grinding his teeth and shouting at the top of his lungs. He will also pinch you on your skin in uncomfortable ways. He will also pinch your last nerves, but here's the thing, he is the kind of person most people will avoid because of his appearance; because of his so-called disability and that kills me. It kills me because he is wonderful man. I knew him as a boy but I am sure he has grown to be man who is just as worthwhile to know as I knew him then.

CHAPTER 8

Street Prophets

Betty Sue Brewster was a professor of mine in grad school. I took a class with her called "Life Amongst the World's Urban Poor." In that class she challenged all of her students to do two poverty experiences. This chapter chronicles one of the two experiences I did that quarter. In addition to her challenge, we had a guest speaker, Andy Bales, who also challenged us to spend a night on Skid Row. He said if we did it, then he would do the experience with us too. Andy was the CEO of the LA Rescue Mission that is on San Julian Street in Skid Row. This made the experience even more exciting and intentional.

Surreal. It is the word that comes to mind when I think of our overnight experience. Our time at Skid Row was like a dream. I kept thinking, "Did that really happen? Were we really just there? Did we actually just sleep there?" The surrealism does not lie in the concept of being at the much-acclaimed Skid Row in itself. It is not the idea of being there, but rather, the surrealism is found in the hard-to-describe feeling that the streets cast on you. It's catching a glimpse of life on the streets for just one night. It is reflecting on how does homelessness affect the people for whom this is an everyday reality?

How does one describe this feeling? Hmmm? Sleeplessness is the best phrase that I could come up with. There is this sense that no one ever fully falls asleep on Skid Row at night. The closest thing I can liken this feeling is the sensation I have on airplanes when I travel.

I am one of those people who can never fully fall asleep on plane rides. This is unfortunate, seeing that I have been on several 10+ hour flights. The sensation I feel is that I cannot quite get past the doors of REM sleep. At best, I can walk through the first step of the threshold of REM but then I am suddenly jolted out of it because of some external or internal factors I cannot always explain. The sensation also feels like my times in New York City in the summer. Every summer as a kid I would live in Far Rockaway Queens. In Far Rockaway my cousins Troy, Stephanie, Andre, Steven, Melonie, Judine, and I would stay up really late at night on the porch, just hanging out.

It was part and parcel of the environment. Essentially, everyone and their mother stayed up late. There was a sense that no one ever went to bed because there was always something going on. This sensation is magnified greatly, with an electricity if you will, as I think of some of the nights we would spend in downtown- in Manhattan. However, with this particular sensation, during my summers in New York, there was at least a sense of excitement and adventure to it.

In Skid Row, however, there was this similar sensation but it was laced with an undergirding feeling of fatalism and hypervigilance. For some people there is a continuous party going on. "Let's live it up while we still have the time" seemed be one of the themes of the night. Such individuals will go and go until they were greeted with a near and coming crash that would end their festivities. And for others there is an exaggerated watchfulness and a numbing fear that will not allow them to sleep. It is the sense that you have to keep one eye opened- whether it is physical, spiritual, mental, or emotional. In this case even if one eye is physically closed your subconscious was always awake.

There is another part to the surrealism. There were some truly peaceful moments on the streets too. The description of its true nature, in its most authentic form, evades me. The best I can say was that I knew God was with us and that fear was not a part of the equation. This was especially evident when talking with the various peaceful souls we met over the course of our stay.

For instance, when I talked to Kareem, a friend I met on San Pedro, I totally forgot where I was. Talking to him was as though I was talking to my grandfather in many ways. And when I say grandfather, I don't mean a figurative person (or an example of) but he truly had aspects that reminded of my own grandfather, my mom's dad. His spirit was so meek and so soft-spoken in nature that it commanded my attention. In effect, it calmed me of any awareness of my surroundings. I remembered talking to Kareem, and for that moment, I totally forgot that I was on Skid Row. I felt like the whole night was filled with pockets of such persons- people of peace. And with these people there was a sense of serendipitous tranquility that came in many forms...

Have you ever had a moment in your life where someone said something to you that you couldn't forget? A moment where their words became echoes that seem to linger beyond that time? Words that have a Deja vu quality? I know I have. When I was in high school, tenth grade I believe, there was a youth pastor that visited my church. There must have been some special meeting going on and he was given the platform to speak to our congregation. At the end of his time he spoke to people individually. He gave words of encouragement and wisdom. I was one of those individuals he spoke to.

I cannot remember what this man looked like at all. It's weird because I usually can remember that sort of thing. I can't remember his appearance but I can easily remember his words. He said many things to me in that time but one particular thought never seemed to escape me. In a prophetic type of way he warned me about the power of listening with spiritual ears. He said that I needed to be diligent. I was to be prepared to hear God speak in very unconventional ways and by unexpected means.

He said, "You might be at bus stop and a random stranger will start talking to you. At first it may seem like rambling, but through humility and understanding you might realize that God might be speaking to you through this person." He then went on to give other examples of how God could speak to me in a surprising fashion. Oddly enough, every example he gave me that day has come to pass in my life. This has caused me to be sensitive and much more cognizant of public interactions. Especially where it concerns street prophets.

I want to expound on the person first concept we talked about in the last chapter. I want talk about people experiencing homelessness. Typically such persons would be labeled as 'homeless people' or 'bums'. And unfortunately, those labels have a plethora of negative connotations wrapped around them.

However, the more I have crossed paths, interacted, and/or done life with people experiencing homelessness, the more I have adopted a new way of thinking. Many, not all, of such persons are street prophets. They are messengers disguised in the robes of poverty but are rich in wisdom and the knowledge of the Kingdom of God. I think there's a big misconception of the places where we think God should and ought to be found. Likewise, there is a misunderstanding of who is qualified to be a mouthpiece of God, an oracle of truth, and a prophet. I have often found that God resides on streets and street corners.

I found God many times on the streets, sitting on benches, and from the hearts and mouths of people experiencing homelessness. I am convinced that there are more true prophets living on the streets than those who reside in church offices and church buildings. I don't mean this from a metaphorical, spiritual, mushy gushy sense. I sincerely believe there is a large population of prophets who are hidden in the urban jungles of America. They have a mission from God, words of wisdom, and an understanding of Jesus many of us do not understand- nor care to.

... Right there in the middle of the street Kareem preached to me- he preached reality. He gave me an understanding about poverty and how it is constructed. All of it seemed like it was a living textbook being read to me. He was a street prophet speaking truth. He talked to me of burned bridges and disconnectedness of his family, community, and loved ones. In a very simplistic way he showed me how easily you and I could fall prey to homelessness. He opened my eyes to the riches and abundance that come with having steady, committed, and loving people being present in one's life.

He taught me something about the nature of relationships. One thing I realized from our interaction is that it is very hard to demonize someone once you know their story. Mercy and compassion often overtake the heart when we are softened by hearing someone's thorough and detailed testament of life. Wisdom tempered with compassion, mercy, and an honest, listening ear will reveal that the outer shell of a human does not reveal the whole picture of who that human is like. Similar to Judd, I saw Jesus in Kareem. And the great thing was that there were more people we met that night that were beautiful and prophetic too.

On that night I decided to make a little list of the people (and situations) that we met during our overnight experience. I decided to utilize the list as a way to remember, connect, and pray for the people we met. More specifically, to remember all the people and situations that occurred that evening. The way I recorded it was to jot down the information on the palm of my hand. It was fitting that I did this because it reminded me that Our Father has all of Skid Row (and all of this world for that matter) in the palm of His hand. He is the best person to bring hope and healing to His children. Whether we believe it or not, He loves us all.

We met other people that night. The following are just a few. Deborah was one of the first persons we talked to on the streets. She began by talking with Andy. She spoke to him about the best ways to help improve Skid Row. In hearing her conversation you could tell she had plenty of concerns about a lot of things. What I loved about her was that she was unafraid to confront the CEO of the Rescue Mission and she demanded answers from him.

There was also Kareem, the man I spoke of before. He had the most profound effect on me- in a positive way. He was a friend of Deborah. They possibly were a couple. He was a man who moved from Chicago to California to avoid his family seeing him in the distraught state he was in due to drugs. And there was also Doc the Musician. He had such a beautiful soul. He loved, loved, loved music. We had a great conversation about Jesus, life, and helping people in Skid row. He also asked us why we were there. That was funny to me because he wasn't the only one who asked this question.

In fact, many people could tell we were not people of the streets. A few times we were asked the same question. Why are you here? And what are you doing? We were honest about our reasons. Upon answering, the disposition of most people was to look out for us. Most told us to be safe and not to end up there permanently.

Then there was Milton who mumbled a lot. He was a representation of several people who also mumbled. I can't explain why but there were many people mumbling to themselves, to the air, or to others. The mumbling spoke to my soul. It led me pray and to take action. My eyes were opened to a unique type of loneliness.

By far the most heart-wrenching thing to watch that night, was a woman I saw dancing all night. It was interesting to note that for most of the night she was only about thirty paces away from our group. At first it came as a beautiful thing to me that she was enjoying herself in the midst of the chaos that encompassed her, but after three hours of dancing it hit me. The dancing did not seem as jovial as I first perceived it. It went from fun-looking and celebratory, to looking like a dance of captivity. This woman was being held captive by a force beyond her reasoning, capability to control, or even be cognizant of.

Whatever drugs she was given or whatever spiritual oppression she was under, it did not sit well with her. She could not stop dancing, even if she wanted to. Her body was captivated by oppression in the worse way. It seemed like she was powerless to choose. Some of the other acts that she committed, I will not mention here because I want to maintain her sense of dignity. It was a shock to the system though. It was hard to believe that someone would do some of things she did in the public eye. The sense of shame or care seemed to evade and be evaporated from her life. Or quite the reverse, maybe the shame had enveloped her life so much that she has lost all ability to care.

This recurring incidence of this woman dancing was the picture I saw over and over in my mind throughout the night. With every attempt I took to fall asleep on the streets I kept seeing her over and over again in my mind. Every time I tried to sleep my thoughts landed on her and her situation. With a heart heavy for her I prayed. I prayed, "Kyrie eleison. Lord, have mercy. Bring peace to her. Bring restoration, Abba. You came to set the captives free."

Before settling into our evening quarters on San Julian Street on Skid Row, we had an opportunity to check out the view of the city from the rooftop. What a breathtaking sight it was. Talk about eye candy. I had done this same thing before, a few years ago, but never had I done it at night. What beauty to behold! As I took in the view I was captivated. We were all captivated. There is nothing like having a feast for the eyes, but even as we were doing this I was confronted with a choice. In fact, we all were. I could keep my eyes up high, along the level of the skyline, or I could let my gaze fall and embrace the juxtaposition that was nestled a little bit lower in my view.

For as my friends and I lowered our gaze we were confronted with Skid Row in all of its totality. The totality was hard to take in. The totality included many people experiencing homelessness, loneliness, and urine streaming from the corner of a generator to the sidewalk and then on to the street. There were tents galore, shady activity, laughter, continual sounds of police sirens, continual speeding of vehicles down the street. There was chatter, music, hope in unexpected forms, bodies lying all over the pavement, trash dispersed everywhere. There were also sounds of distress, genuine care, genuine despair, fear, and rats darting to and fro.

It was a lot of stimulation to take in. Indeed, there were good, or at least relatively good, things that we saw going on the streets. However, in the parallel comparison to the beauty of the skyline, it was hard to see it. It was difficult to see what lay beyond the borders of the Row. We were confronted with incarnation. We had a dilemma. Should we keep our eyes away from the troublesome things and situations? Should we gaze only upon beauty? Should we ignore what is painful and oppressive? Should we shut our ears? Close our eyes? Stay on the mountain? Should we sleep on the rooftop? And not sleep on the streets?

Ultimately we made the choice to stay on the streets that night. We slept on Skid Row. And because of it my interactions with people experiencing homelessness have dramatically changed. Here and there I have gained brothers and sisters I would have otherwise not had. And I am growing in my understanding of the pulpit and the platform that the street possess. I became more aware that Jesus would fit in better amongst those experiencing homelessness than those who are rich. There is a power in poverty. There is a reason Jesus says blessed are the poor because the kingdom belongs to them.

CHAPTER 9

Supernatural

Can I ask you a question? Or two? What do you feel about demons, angels, and the supernatural realm? Do you think such things exist or do you think these entities only belong to the realms of fantasy, movies, myths, and literature? Let me give you a minute to think about it.

Did you answer yes, no, or maybe? Tell me. I want to know. Well, for me, I cannot exclude the existence of the supernatural realm because it is undeniable within my own life experiences. Without hesitation, I would readily answer the previous sets of questions with a sound yes. In my life the supernatural realm has been as equally active as the physical realm. Many of you reading this might agree with that statement, but I am willing to bet that there might be just as many of you reading this who might find such thoughts as far-fetched or asinine. For those with the later sentiment, I can only tell you what I have experienced. I will let you decide for yourself if it is true. If you are still up for it, let me tell you a story or two about finding my Father in the supernatural.

As I share, there will be no posturing to convince you of my theological or philosophical beliefs. Rather, I ask for an opportunity for you to hear a different part of my story. Nonetheless, I might have to give you a little bit of a background in order for you to understand my thinking. This is a chapter that many people around the world can resonate with. This is particularly true if you are reading this from a non-Western background or nontraditional in your upbringing. But if you live in the Western world or Northwestern Hemisphere, this might be a stretch in your linear thinking.

Ecclesiastes 3 is a passage in the Bible that speaks about the powerful entity of time. It relates to its hearers the message that there is a time for everything thing under the sun. There is a time to live and a time to die, a time to dance and a time to mourn, and a time to plant and time to pluck up what is planted. These are but a few of the time pairings that the author mentions.

He also mentions that there is time for war and a time for peace. I believe this to be a true statement. Albeit, what I believe about war and peace is more centered on the spiritual realm than the physical realm. I believe there is greater battle going on in the *unseen* than that which is *seen* in our world. I believe there is more than meets the eye when it comes to human struggles. Our struggles are not merely stress, strain, violence, and oppression that we can experiences solely with our 5 senses. Yes, those are very real, but I also believe the battles we face spiritually, emotionally, and psychologically are just as real.

I believe we are in daily war, whether we know it or not. Whether we acknowledge it, or not, I believe it exists. Unfortunately, I think we are generally numb to this aspect of our world. Quite simply, we just can't see it.

I don't like to take spiritual warfare and the supernatural realm lightly. So much so, that I have opted out of watching scary movies for the purposes of entertainment. When people ask me why I don't watch horror films I usually tell them I have experienced things in real life that mirror some of what is being portrayed in theaters.

For me, it is hard to justify watching a portrayal of someone's demonic misery as a form of entertainment. I have seen enough real life manifestations of evil and torment that I can't justify watching such movies for fun and enjoyment. This is also true for me when comes to movies with torment, excessive gore, and twisted revenge. Let's just say I am not a fan of Quentin Tarantino movies, the *Saw* serious, *Paranormal Activities*, or *Purge* series.

I don't know why but I have had several periods in my life when spiritual activity was stronger than normal. I can't tell if it is a cycle or a random set of seasons. In these moments, whether they are weeks or months, there is always a direct encounter with the spiritual realm. In these periods of time I would have run-ins with angelic activity. Sometimes it would be the positive type of angelic activity, but more often the activity would be demonic in nature. There have been quite a few times myself and a prayer partner would be lead to cast out demons and deal with evil spirits. Yep, you read that correctly.

During college, I had one of those periods where God was doing some pretty spectacular things. My best friend, Anthony and I, encountered some outrageously dynamic moments back then. These were moments where we only could attribute the happenings as something divinely inspired. For months God would show up in strange ways. You probably wouldn't believe some of things He did unless you were there. Especially, the things He did in the dorms. Especially, during the second semester of my sophomore year. That is where the fun happened.

I remembered that we were woken up plenty of times by God during those days. You see, Anthony and I, we were roommates during that year. We had a bunk bed style set up. At the time I was on the bottom bunk and he was the top bunk. Like random clock work, we both would be awakened out of our sleep with an incredible burning to pray. Prayer was always the thing that led us into these powerful moments. Whether we were pacing back and forth, on our knees in reverence, or prostrate in tears on the floor, fervent prayer was always involved.

In these times we both would acknowledge if the other person was awake before we began praying aloud. In those moments we would pray silently or quietly to ourselves. Inevitably, one of us would ask the other, "Hey, are you awake? What is God saying to you? " This was almost always the case. The other person was lying awake waiting to hear from God.

We both could sense the presence of God in those moments. We both understood that God was speaking clearly to us. Without hesitation, instantly we both would end up praying. And what would happen next would always be interesting. Often times we both would have a particular person that God would place on our hearts. These were students from the dorms. We would pray for these individuals or for some particular prayer need that was connected to them.

What got to be real interesting is when some of those same individuals would come knocking on our doors. Many times, they would come knocking just after we started praying for them. Or we would go and find them and pray for them ourselves. Without fail, everyone of one those prayers ended up in a divine appointment. It was like God had set up the whole thing. Many times it would end up like this. Some guy from the dorm would knock on our door and say something like, "Hey guys, I really need some prayer," or "I really just need someone to talk to," or "I have this problem...."

These encounters would begin with talking. Thereafter, we would have something close to a counseling session. Inevitably, the conversation would end in some form of pronounced freedom or deliverance. It was something God Himself orchestrated. We could never take credit for anything that transpired.

Probably the most memorable moment of this kind was an encounter that happened about a year later. During that time I was an RA, a Resident Assistant, in the same dorm, but this time Anthony and I lived as neighbors. We were across the hall from each other.

It was a Sunday night. The kind of Sunday night at college where you don't want the weekend to end. It was the type of Sunday where you squeezed in as much fun as possible because you know Monday is coming with exams. At that time I knew I should have been studying. After all, pre-med prerequisites for medical school couldn't be completed on their own. However, I just needed a few more minutes to chill. So, what did I do? I headed over to best friend Anthony's room to see if he "needed" a study break.

In the process, I ran into a fellow leader who lived in another dorm. He was knocking on Anthony's door. He seemed very earnest in his knocking. He had a sort of desperation in his voice, his eyes, and overall demeanor. He seemed anxious for help. Anthony opened the door but he didn't seem to be in the mood to talk to anyone at the time. He had just started to fall asleep. He also had that rushed look, like, "I ought to be heading to bed or studying right now." He stood in the doorway finding the words to turn this guy away but then it hit both of us. We realized this was a moment we couldn't let go by.

Like prior scenarios such as this, we sat and started to listen to this young man. His story was compelling. He told us stories of abuse, trauma, gang violence, more abuse, painful relationships, and what sounded like occult activities. Right away we knew this was going to be a different kind of night. He continued telling us story after story. And he expressed to us that he had trouble sleeping. He felt like his soul was being tormented. This was the point where we offered prayer.

Now that we had the experience of previous demonic encounters, we felt very comfortable in exorcising. In some ways it was actually rather enjoyable. I mean, isn't always a great thing to have chains loosen in one's life?

There was something completely different with this encounter than the others we had before. The evil spirits connected to him had no real desire to let him go. In fact, it was a monumental struggle to see him get free. He started manifesting. Pretty much, he started doing some of the things you would expect in an exorcists movie. He had the contorted voice. The spirits attached to him tried to threaten us. He writhed in anguish but didn't do the whole levitation thing or vomit profusely.

The struggle was real. We finally came to an impossible impasse in the deliverance session. There was this still and hushed moment where we realized there was nothing we could do from our current capabilities. We had never faced resistance like this before. I remembered Anthony and I looked at each other with a kind of exhausted concern. We both wondered what to do beyond that point. I remembered us praying and asking God for wisdom and direction. I remembered God was clear in this moment. He said, "Don't worry, I will handle this myself." And then it got really weird in biblical proportions. A scene out of the Bible literally transpired right in front of our eyes.

So you have to get this picture. The young man was sitting in a chair about 3 feet away from the both of us. Anthony and I were about a few feet from each other pacing and praying. And then we became still. I kid you not. And I know some of you are not going to believe this, but it really did happen. Halfway between us there was a Presence. And that Presence was Jesus.

The reason I know this is because there was a dialogue with the young man and Jesus. Although we couldn't see or hear Jesus out loud we could clearly hear what the spirits in this guy were saying. It was a page directly out of the Bible. Like the story about the man with Legion of demons, the guy in the chair started pleading with Jesus. He begged in a desperate voice, "Jesus, is it time already? Have you come to judge us?" This is what he said.

And then what transpired afterwards was a dialogue of bargaining. What resulted in the end was that Jesus Himself delivered this this young man. We just stood there in pure humility and watched and heard half of a dialogue in deliverance. When this guy was delivered and Jesus drove out the spirits, the young man collapsed to the floor. He crumpled to the floor, but not in a bad or painful way. It was more like a release. He actually looked rather peaceful and graceful as he slumped to the floor. His demeanor went from struggle and strain to utter peace.

It was so nice to see him in a place of rest. He was so at peace that we left him right there on the floor. We let him sleep right there in there on the ground throughout the night. With every breath you could see that a heavy load had been lifted off his shoulder. We had witness something incredible that night. We had sought and found God in a war zone. It sounds like an unlikely place to find Jesus. However, Jesus is all things and in all things. Included in his names, we found that Jesus is a lover *and* a fighter.

We found out that there are some battles that Jesus Himself handles in his own way with no human striving required. In these times we are to sit back, stand back, and behold his handiwork in bringing about liberty to the captive, broken-hearted, and bound. In these moments we just stand still and know that He is God.

CHAPTER 10

My Skin

Bear with me. You have just entered a realm that is filled with many streams of thought. They are streams that lead to one river. It is a river that speaks to a particular set of experiences in Uganda. It captures a snapshot of my time in Uganda as well seeking and finding God in and underneath my skin. It's strange to think about it, but God is found in my melanin and underneath it too. I have never thought that deeply about this being true until I had my two excursions in Uganda. What a place to learn that!

If you have read this far in my book, then I feel compelled to say something to you as a tangential thought. This next statement is a standalone statement that I think you need to hear. Please make *no mistake* in hearing it and receiving it. Here it is:

Accidents may have happened in your life. Maybe more than what seems normal. Mistakes and losing things may seem like a common occurrence that is attached to your life. And you might have come to believe that you are a mistake. However, you are not an accident. You might feel like you are cursed. Like you are doomed to fail. Or that your life is destined for the worst track possible. Listen to me. It's not true. You were made on purpose and with an intentional purpose. This statement is real. This statement, my friends, is true. Your life is worthwhile and meaningful...

Growing up I hated the phrase accident-prone. Even writing those words right now makes me uneasy and low-key angry. I especially loathed the phrase coming from the lips of my family members. This is my family on my maternal side. As a collective my family deemed me the accident-prone person of our family. Unbeknownst to me is the reason why. I don't know why these random things always seemed to happen to me. And they always seem to happen to me, especially in the presence of my family.

What sucks is that I couldn't blame my family for calling me that name because to a degree it was true. I couldn't begin to tell you all the accidents and mishaps that have occurred to me. Accidents have had a funny way of following me. Random rocks would fly my way and hit me in the middle of a crowd. I am that guy that hits the median in the middle of the road and gets two flat tires when others wouldn't. And my injuries are typically random. They are typically concurrent with bad timing. One of the best examples of this truth comes from the constant chipping of my two front teeth.

The most humorous experience of my accident-prone part of my life has to be with my two front teeth. I have chipped and/ or broken one or both of my two front teeth at least five times. Those five times happened in five different ways and in five different locations.

The first time I chipped my teeth was probably the most traumatizing. In that incident I ran through a glass window on Halloween. There will be more on that story later in this chapter. My second time happened at Camp Barnabas. As a camp counselor, I was showing a bad example, by walking up a water slide instead of going down the water slide. As a result I slammed my head face first on the slide and promptly chipped my teeth.

I chipped my tooth again, and for a third time, by eating some barbecue ribs. Now that one was quite random. I was just minding my own business and then all of a sudden ... *Chip*. Then, oddly, and unfortunately, I redesigned my tooth once more by eating sugar cane in Jamaica the day before my father's funeral. It was so strange. The worst part was introducing myself to family members I have never met, while simultaneously trying to hide my chipped tooth. That was a draining and humorous task.

And finally, the fifth and most recent chipping happened at the monastery in Taizé. It's the one I mentioned earlier. The one in the middle of the countryside of France. What had happened was.... I had eaten a stale baguette. *A very stale one.* I can remember vividly, the crunchy sound that lead me to reveal to my friends that part of my tooth was missing. Again.

I have to say though, the first time I chipped my tooth was the best of them all. You see, that one has a funny story to it. That one happened on Halloween. In particular, it was the first Halloween that I would officially go trick-or-treating, and subsequently it was the last. LOL!

Candy was the reason why I got hurt that night. It was all that was on my mind that evening. I was so excited to collect as many pieces of those diabetes-inducing objects as I could. However, that excitement and enthusiasm definitely got the better of me. The consequence of it all was that my knee and two front teeth paid a price.

You see, I was bouncing around my house in excitement. In this rapturous moment of ecstasy I bounded around the house, running freely and wildly. I was doing this while also trying to be "semi" responsible. After all, my duty for that evening was to close all the windows and the doors in the house in order to depart on my candy excursion.

So overcome with joy, I ran towards the back door of my house. In between the door that I wanted to close and my living room, there was an infamous glass window. A clean and clear glass window. For some reason on that night the window was extra clean and extra see-through. Key term: *extra*. I say that because the way I ran through it was as if I could jump through it. And let me tell you, I could not.

The funny thing about it is I didn't feel anything until I talked to my grandmother. At the time she was in her room. It was only then that I noticed it all. The blood. The gashed knee that I had. The chipped teeth that were present. I was quickly rushed to the Urgent Care in Pembroke Pines. My Auntie Olive was the person who would help and comfort me. I remembered her being very task-oriented in the "waiting room." I put the words waiting room in quotes because with her around I didn't have to wait much at all.

It's funny because I have seen her in this mode many times when any person goes to the hospital in our family. She doesn't mess around. She made sure the doctors gave me the best treatment and that I was seen as quickly as possible. She made sure that I was more than just ok. She insisted that I was treated well. Honestly, I had the best royal treatment from that experience. And I want to say I really appreciated that moment...

If you know me at all you would know that I forget things, misplace things, and can't always remember the most important objects in my life. Keys, wallets, passports, licenses, and important documents are all fair game to go missing in my life. Although frustrating, these missing objects have definitely added a richness to my life. I have grown to become less stressed when I lose things because it has happen to me so many times that I don't panic. All objects have a capability to be found, replaced, or lost.

In fact, my second trip to Uganda started with a missing passport. Literally the day and night before we needed to leave for Uganda I misplaced my passport. It was the most nerve wracking, upsetting, and frustrating experience. The search for the passport started early in the morning and it ended late in the evening. I should have known by the missing passport that our trip was not going to be smooth sailing like my first time I visited Uganda.

My travel companion for the trip was a student of mine from Barnabas Prep. His name was Tomas Swenson. Barnabas Prep is a college-like preparatory program for adults with disabilities. It was an extension of Camp Barnabas and its aim and focus was to help students transition from post high school into an everyday adulthood. We did this through learning life skills, job skills, and applying resources in everyday living.

Tomas was one my favorite students in the program. He became an incredibly dear brother to me. If you were to meet him, I am sure you would be inspired by him. He is really smart, extremely diligent, loyal, and a very hard worker. He happens to have a visual impairment, which honestly is overshadowed by how incredible his abilities shine through.

Back to the story with the passport. We were leaving the next day and I couldn't find it. So, I employed my housemate Nate, Tomas, and myself to the task. We were the people doing the search for my wallet. And I swear to you (I probably shouldn't do that), we searched high and low for that friggin' passport. When I say we searched. We sincerely looked everywhere. I am talking about looking in places we probably didn't need to. Examples are the freezer of the fridge, the oven, and the dishwasher. Yes, the dishwasher!

And then there was the couch in the living room. Bruh. I can't tell you the sweat and swearing I did in and on my head. I can't tell you how many times I looked in, on, around, and through this couch. I tell you the truth, I looked in the couch a million times to try and find my passport. I speak with utter hyperbole. So did Nate. So did Tomas.

But guess who found my passport that night? In the dark? With minimal lighting? Feeling his way through the darkness it was Tomas that came and saved the day. It was a bit ironic as Tomas touted himself. He said the obvious thought we were all thinking. He said, "Isn't it crazy that the blind guy was the one who found the passport?" It was very humorous and fitting indeed.

That marked the beginning of our hilarious adventure to Uganda. It was another trip that was bonkers in every way imaginable. In another occasion I will have to tell you more about Tomas and our adventure. Losing the wallet was just the tip of the iceberg for us. For now though, I want to tell you about my first trip to Uganda, because it ties in the randomness that I mentioned earlier in this chapter.

I know it might seem odd, but the stories I spoke of at the beginning of this chapter are not random. The stories in combination speak of a mentality I have had to face and fight all of my life and I suspect that many of you reading this have felt the same way too! You see, under the layers of my dark brown skin, that I wear, is a mental battle. It's been going on for years. The untruths that I have faced are vicious lies that love to wreak havoc in my mind during moments of weakness and depression. The message that I have received in one way or another is this: You are a mistake; you are prone to fail; you are not valuable; no one cares for you; and no one would miss you if you were gone. You are a forgotten child. You are dark, but not lovely.

Uganda had a wonderful way of surprising me continuously. One of the most pleasant surprises that I experienced was the healing of my skin condition. It was not a complete healing but a degree of healing. Now you might be asking, "What condition am I speaking of?" The condition of being black in the States. The condition of having dark-skin in America.

Now, when I say healing, I simply mean that I can now say this with confidence: "I love being a dark-skinned, brown, black man!" Being dark is an incredible blessing! You see, while in Uganda, I was afforded the opportunity to step away from the negative imagery of blackness in the States. And I was granted the gift of embracing the loveliness of being dark-skinned.

My experience in Uganda shed light on an inner conflict. In the States, at the subconscious level, there is always a war going on within me about my darkness- my blackness. It is not a war that overtly hampers my daily life but nonetheless it is a struggle. In the States I fight against falling prey to the negative stereotypes. The ones that our media portrays of black people- especially of black men. All around me there are tokens of expression that say black equals less than, ignorant, threatening, and dangerous. I know, of course this is not true, but the messages are relentless.

In the States I fight myself about my own skin color. The question I sometimes ask is this: Am I black enough? There are often times where I have not felt black enough for other black people. In particular, among those who are of my own skin color, I have been cited as being too white. Or better yet, "You sound white." What does that mean? And what does that mean about what makes a black person black? Does it go beyond the skin color?

Conversely, among white people, sometimes I am too black. This is rare, though. In some cases my blackness comes as a liability, a threat, and a not welcomed feature. Seeing past my character, there have been some who have made judgments solely on my skin color and in the same breath, some white people, also don't think I am black enough. They quote me as not, "being like other black people," or, "You are not *really* black." They relegate me to having the Oreo Syndrome. You know, black on the outside, white on the inside. As an "Oreo" I wouldn't be classified as one of "those" black people- the ones that we see on television or hear on the radio. This further perpetuates the negative imagery.

To make it a little more complicated, let's throw in one more thing. In the States there is also an awkwardness I have because of my ethnic heritage as well. I am a Jamaica-born man who was raised in South Florida, and I grew in a suburban-ish environment with my Jamaican grandparents. Due to this complexity, I have also run into multiple issues because of the cultural differences in my blackness.

However, like I said, these issues are not extremely detrimental to my daily life. It is mostly an inward conflict that chips away at my soul. The damage is an inner angst that has primarily affected my identity. The chief problem is that I cannot fully appreciate my dark skin as I would like to. However, Uganda, changed a lot of that. Being in an African nation was a freeing experience! There, my blackness or rather my brownness, was honored, appreciated, and dare I say- normal. I loved that!

In Uganda, from my first step, I entered into a whole new worldview of my darkness. For starters, it was the most incredible feeling to be engulfed in sea of dark-skinned people. It was the first time in a very long time where I was a part of the majority. And I don't mean Atlanta majority; I mean *errybody* was black. Like 99.79 percent. The exception would be places of heavy Western or Asian influence like the city of Jinja.

Everywhere we went there were all shades of dark skin. Consequently, I quickly became comfortable in my own skin. In fact it made me wonder, is this how white people feel on a daily basis in the States? Comfortable? Relaxed? At home? I'm not gonna lie. It was kind of nice to just melt away in the crowd for a few minutes, hours, days, weeks. Just to be one of the many brown people. Normal. Typical. Not a minority. Not an aberration.

Although I did like that feeling, the real healing came from living and doing life with my Ugandan brothers and sisters. In Uganda I experienced almost the complete opposite of my inner battle in the States. In Uganda, my brothers and sisters took my blackness as an automatic commonality. It was a positive thing. Right away they said, "Welcome home." There was so much meaning in that. I cannot begin to tell you how much that meant.

There is a holistic wave of peace and wholeness that a black person feels when they return to an African nation. Especially, when they return home for the first time. Coming home feels good. I was at home. I felt at home. I truly belonged. I did not have to work for it. I did not have to prove anything. I was dark-skinned and that was good enough.

What made this even more delightful was that my Ugandan family gave me a Ugandan name. In fact they gave me two names: Mugerwa and Mutasa. Mugerwa means "mighty warrior" and Mutasa was a king. There will be more about the name significances in another story at another time, but let's says it was more than just an expression of mere kindness. They treated me according to my name and it was a reminder that I was a part of something bigger and grander.

In Uganda I was floored by the character of dark skinned people everywhere I went. This place did not follow the protocol of Western media. Everywhere I went, both in the Christian community and other communities, I was greeted by people who dismantled the American stereotype of black people- in particular black men. And in particular African people. In Ugandan I experienced hospitality so wonderful that I could cry. There were black angels everywhere. Almost everywhere we went people were so kind, so open, so giving and so loving.

People were incredibly welcoming and they were so gracious and loving to foreigners- those who looked different than themselves. My teammates on my trip were all white but they were treated so well. People gave them their babies to hold, their homes to live in, and their hearts to share, even without knowing them fully. I'm sure if we looked further into the fabric of Ugandan culture we would see some of the negatives as well but I was too overwhelmed by the goodness to notice it.

In particular, the brown men that I met in Kampala and Jinja were full of utmost integrity and humility. They had such incredible character. The men I met were men who thought way beyond themselves. They were generational in their thinking. Some of these men reminded me of the men in my church I attended during my childhood. In their hearts and in their actions, they were concerned about generations. Their minds were on the well-being and prosperity of their nation and their children's children's children. Their hands, work, and actions matched what they believed. They lived far above and greater than the pettiness of that we Americans live for today!

These men were true fathers. Not only were they fathers to their own biological children but they were fathers to the fatherless. Their scope of family and togetherness was unrivaled. And the wisdom that the possessed was akin to the lineage of Solomon. As a man who grew up without my father, my heart was beyond filled with joy and admiration. These men were and are my heroes. Subsequently, day after day, I grew to love my skin color more and more because these men and women were living a life that I aspired to live.

All in all, I left Uganda proud! I was proud to be black (brown). I was proud to be a Christ-follower. Although my primary identity is a son of God and Christ-follower, it was definitely a nice bonus to enjoy my skin color too!

It was such a blessing to be around great people. In general, it was great to know that there are men and women of God doing great things across the seas. But it was extra special, in this particular time of my life, to see that these people were ones with dark skin. They were people, people with my own skin color, that were peeling away the stereotypes, prejudices, and misconceptions that pervade throughout many societies of the world. Mainly one's touched with the cruelty found in pre-, post-, and neo-colonialism. There is so much more I can say on the subject but I will stop here for now. I am very grateful for this healing and blessing. It was so simple and yet so profound. I sought and found God in another way foreign to me. I sought and found Him in and under my skin.

This leads me to ask you a poignant set of questions. I would like for you to answer these questions for yourself. And then one day, let us talk about it face to face, by email, or by some other means of communication. Here it is:

Are you comfortable in your own skin? Do like all the features that God has given you? Have you sought and found God in and underneath your skin?

CHAPTER 11

Mountain

I am pretty sure that most people would agree that being stuck in traffic is not an enjoyable task to have in our lives. Most often we see it is a necessary evil. It is something that we have learned to manage in our day-to-day routines. In fact, many of us have learned how to manage this frustration through coping mechanisms.

Some of us cope in traffic by practicing language skills. For instance, some of us brush up on our "sign language" during these times of traffic. I'm sure this is where most of us have learned to use the "birdy" as a consistent communication method. And others of us work on our "foreign language skills" during this time. In these moments we speak a lot of "French" to our neighbors who cut us off. However, this time can be enjoyable too. The traffic can also lead to some soothing moments of comedy and meditation. For instance, whenever I am stuck in traffic I can always count on one thing to make me smile and bring me serenity. Bumper stickers!

Yes, I know. You can roll your eyes all you want, but I like them. Especially the tacky ones that are spread out on junky-looking vehicles. I know this sounds juvenile and trivial but I think they are great. And although I would never have them on my own car, they are hella amusing to see on other vehicles.

There is one type of bumper sticker that I like the most. I am especially fond of the ones that talk about where the driver "would rather be." These stickers usually read like, "I'd rather be... fishing, dirt biking, mud wrestling, crocheting, kissing my pet, etc." Without a doubt, they are typically hilarious to read. And at the same time, these little stickers have the power to be revealing and symbolic. They bring about a small microcosm of the owner's personality and passions. The stickers speak to the type of things that they are into, fight for, hate, or love.

Like with all things, even bumper stickers can bring me to a reflective place. Bumper stickers, like the ones I mentioned before, beg me to ask the question of myself. Where would I rather be? On any given day, if you were to ask me where I rather be, I would readily have two answers to give to that question. I would either say near an ocean or on a mountain. Hands down. Why? Well, both can be breathtaking. Both are vast and beautiful. Both command my attention. Both are scary and yet inviting. Both possess unknowns. Both give me a truer perspective about life and who I am. They both teach me to honor and respect my place on this earth. And both are undeniably incredible places to seek and find God.

The mountains though, have a particular and special place in my heart because the mountains have taught me lessons that the ocean has not. At least not yet. The mountains have one element that continues to captivate me. The mountains have always delivered on this one thing the higher I have climbed them. That one thing is....

I have had many experiences on mountains. I have climbed up to Half Dome in Yosemite with a small group of seven. I have regularly traversed several sets of mountain trails on the San Gabriel range. And I would probably say that the Echo Mountain Trail and Chantry Flats are my favorite go-to spots to visit when

I lived in SoCal. Above all of my mountain experiences, there is a unique fondness that I have with my most recent experience. It is a time that I shared with my students and staff mates from Touching Miami with Love. It was a trip laden with unforgettable times of "firsts."

I don't think I have mentioned this to you yet, but I currently work as a Youth Coordinator at TML. I cannot begin to tell you all that TML offers to the community in Overtown, but let's just say this: we are definitely multilayered in our approach, outreach, and reciprocal relationships and partnerships. My specific role at TML is working with our Youth in an afterschool program. My job entails working directly with Middle and High School students in Overtown. The work itself is a mission of teaching students life skills that will help them be prepared for life after high school. The effort is holistic in nature. Our programs focus on the growth of students physically, spiritually, mentally, socially, emotionally, and academically. A part of tackling this challenge is to provide experiences to students that will help them become confident both inside and outside of the environments they grew up in.

Touching Miami with Love is located in Overtown. Overtown would be considered a part of the inner city of Miami, Florida. It has a reputation that typically is associated with poverty, crime, drugs, brokenness, and pain. On first glance it would be known to have the vestiges of what you would find in a common "hood" of America. Such cities are places that are propagated and continued by greed, lack of empathy, systemic oppression, and internal cultural conflict.

That's mostly what you would hear or think of Overtown if you were to follow the news or get the hearsay. And it also would be true to some degree depending on the day, time, or area in Overtown. Admittedly, some of the hype and negative imagery cannot be denied. The good, the bad, and the ugly do coexist in the Town. Fortunately, there is another narrative running through Overtown. That narrative is a narrative of resilience and resistance. This narrative belongs to the rising generation found in the hearts of Overtown and neighboring cities like it. I find that narrative most clearly in my students who are growing up in and around Overtown. Not only have I seen that narrative in Overtown, but I have seen that narrative unfold on a mountain in Yosemite.

This resilience I speak of was displayed and found in 9 high school students, 1 middle school student, and 1 recent high school graduate. All of whom have faced personal challenges and struggles prior to our trip. The female students' names were Ahmar'a, Breshay, Damary, Selena, Shakayla, and Mckenzie for the girls. The boys' names were Vernon, Jordan, David, Antony, and Gerald. These mountaineers were accompanied by three leaders from our organization, including me. The other leaders were an amazing couple named Gavin and Amanda Knight. They also happened to be my neighbors and friends. We literally live diagonal of each other and in the same apartments.

All fourteen of us participated in an opportunity and an adventure of a lifetime from Miami, Florida to the backcountry of Lower Yosemite in California. Our team joined with an organization called Big City Mountaineers. They are an organization that provides outdoor backpacking experiences and excursions to students that live within inner city environments. Whether it is Colorado, Minnesota or California, many students are provided several destinations to explore nature and become one with the outdoors. I love this organization and its premise.

Once we arrived into California our trip was split into two. The guys went on a separate location to Lower Yosemite. The fellas were led by two volunteers and our lead guide. The volunteers were Jake and Jim. And our lead guide was Dave. They each were wonderful in their own ways. The ladies went to another location in the High Sierras. Both groups encountered phenomenal journeys of firsts. At the very least I know this was true with the guys. I know this story very well because we were together for about a week. And it was an eventful week to say the least.

As mentioned, the trip was a journey of "firsts" for many of our students. This included the fact that many of our students had never been on an airplane before. Let alone, many had not left the state of Florida. So just imagine, the nerves, excitement, and hesitation that the trip presented to each person. We were traveling further than most had ever gone before. And not to mention, we were doing things that most in the group had never thought to do before.

It wasn't just the flight that was a part of our crew's first time happenings. I mean, almost everything was new. It was the first time that many of our students had set up, broke down, and slept in a tent -while living outdoors. Honestly, it was the first time for many of us to be in the wilderness for a prolonged period of time, but the first time experiences didn't end there. Most of our crew had never seen the stars like the way we did. We were free from obstructions. We saw shooting stars and constellations freely, without the city light pollution. We even had many people see snow for the first time, have the pleasure of pooping in the woods for the first time, fish for the first time, *and* even deal with a hail storm for the first time. There are too many first time things to count.

Speaking of hail. One of the most surprising first time experiences that we had was on the first day we went into the backcountry of Yosemite. Let's just say we went through a hail of a time within our first few minutes on the trail. (Knee slapper). We were only on the trail for about 20 minutes before we could hear thunder in the distance. The thunder was soon followed by dark clouds. The clouds were followed by a chilling gust of wind and a prompt temperature drop. We went from summer to winter in a few minutes.

As we started our trek our lead guide, Dave, spoke to us about the abnormality of rain and storms during that time of year. Being the great leader he was, however, he wasn't hesitant to tell us what we should do if we were to encounter a thunderstorm and/ or lightning strikes. This was helpful, because little did we know this would be an abhorrent adventure. It was a trip that had plenty of weather episodes. All of which were deviant from the norm.

In the middle of him explaining to us what to do should we encounter lightning, a chilling breeze rushed in over us. That cold draft was then accompanied with small droplets of rain. The small drops quickly turned into big cold drops of rain. And then the drops changed form altogether. Small bits of hail started to pelt us. We had to take cover. It was a funny sight to behold. We were grown and young men taking desperate cover under trees as hail continued to rain down on us. By the end of it all, the hail grew in size. We became invincible to its pelting pain and simultaneously we grew in our capacity to embrace adventure and new challenges.

It was a blessing in disguise. It felt like the hail storm provided the proper initiation for our journey. Little did we know, the hail storm was just the beginning. It was a perfect start to us facing the many challenges we would meet on the trail. Something interesting to note was that the challenges came in a holistic form. Each challenge tackled a different part of our whole selves. The challenges were mental, physical, spiritual, and emotional and at the same time they taught us something creative about our true selves and our relationship towards God and our teammates. The following are a few of the challenges that we faced.

One of the battles that we had to face right away was limitation. Everyone one on our team had to face it in their own way. This was the battle that happened in between the ears. And in particular, it was battle that most of my students probably struggled with the most.

Questions arose all the time because of mental blocks that constantly barraged us. The questions came in forms of sarcasm and blatant acts of resistance. One of the days we had a small movement, a *morning of resistance*. There were three students who decided for about a half an hour that they didn't want to go hiking that day. At the time this union strike was really frustrating to me as a leader. I could see, however, in this moment the questions were loud and clear. The questions were plaguing us.

The questions were questions of: How long are we hiking for? Why are we doing this? Who does this kind of trip? Do we really have to keep going today? Why can't we just head back home right now? What's the point of this trip? Can I do this? Will we make it? Is it ok for me to fail? The further we travelled, and the more difficult the climb, the questions increased. And the doubts became obvious. It was evident that we struggled with self-confidence, and in our abilities, as we trudged along our trails but- it was fascinating. The questions decreased and the belief increased once we got to the halfway point, reached our first summit, and became more and more used to hiking long miles. Isn't it funny how that works?

I think most of the questions were centered on fear. More specifically the fear of failure. It is a common fear but it is annoying as hell. The other fear we had to fight was the fear of starting something and not completing it. There was a silent whisper amongst all of our souls. The whispered questioned was if we could do all the challenges set before us. We asked ourselves, "Will we give in when the challenges seem unbearable or too hard to complete?"

Now, you have to know that none of these things were said out loud, at least not clearly. And they weren't said right away. After all, our various levels of pride and inability to communicate fear kept us from voicing it at first, but then we had a moment where we confronted these fears. During one of the first sessions around the fire we took time to speak about our fears. And we also spoke about what we wanted to accomplish for that day. We said these words clearly and succinctly and then we wrote them down. We placed them on a yellow flag and we had our navigator of the day carry them in front of us throughout that day. So, whenever we were struggling we would use it as a reference point. That yellow flag became handy for some us that day.

Naturally, our team also dealt with physical challenges. This is something that could not be avoided even if we tried. After all, any great mountain is designed to kill you little by little as you ascend it. The reward for moving towards the top is a beating of your flesh, but the end result is utter exhilaration and joy unspeakable.

On our trip we ascended to nearly 10,000 feet. For a group that consisted of half whom have never traversed a mountain, I was sincerely proud of our progress. I was impressed by our team that we made it. Especially, because it wasn't an easy ride on the way up. We had definitely waded through several waves of complaints, gripes, doubts, breaks and stops, and even anger to make it to the top. In the beginning it was hard to imagine how we would get there but we did. It was amazing.

It was great in other ways too. Ascending a mountain can really tell you a lot about a team and about individuals. Right away we learned which people are leaders, good and bad followers, go-getters, lazy, out of shape, encouragers, along for the ride, comedians, and/or adventurers. We had a little of everything on our team. All of the above. The mountains can really bring a lot out of person and a community. It was so delightful to see this unfold. And it was even more delightful to see the progression that occurred in a short period of time.

One person that stood out to me the most on our trip was our youngest member of our crew. His name was Jordan. I hope he doesn't mind me sharing this but the first part of the trip was a bit abysmal for Jordan. It was rough. I think it was a mixture of things that hit him. It was something he ate, the altitude, the temperature changes, the climbing, the constant ascent, and the heavy hiking packs that we carried.

All of this resulted in a moment of burn out on our first day in the backcountry. On that day he threw up, became a bit faint, and dealt with exhaustion and a bit of ridicule from some teammates. He had the perfect opportunity to quit, be upset, become grouchy, and be bitter. He was none of the above. Instead, Jordan took a moment of rest, recovered, and continued the journey. It was quite amazing. From that day on, Jordan showed me a picture of resiliency that I had not seen in someone of his age in a really long time.

Not only did Jordan make it through that day. He took it to the next level. Every day that we were presented with something new, he wasn't hesitant to try it. In fact, he would take the time to listen first and humbly learn the instruction of what he needed to do. And then with a quiet enthusiasm he would try it.

Between the challenges we faced as a team, the personal challenges I faced as an individual (including a little hypothermia scare), and the sunrise moments that were filled with silence, I sought and found God in a different way than I had not done before. I found God to have a new and bolder character. I found God to be challenging. This is what I concluded with my time: God is like a mountain, the higher you climb in intimacy with Him the more glorious the relationship you have with Him but do not be fooled or miss out on the direct correlation God has with a mountain. Mountains are quite complex.

God is very much the same in this respect. I find that if you want to know Him deeply, purely, and honestly you have climb to the heights that no one wants to scale. You have to place your feet in unknown and uncharted territories. You have to be ok with your feet slipping sometimes.

The path to God's heart and the depths of his love are quite often filled with challenges. Just like the mountain, God depths of love are often found in the unexpected challenges life offers to us. And with it we get the opportunity to be like Jordan. We get to embrace each challenge and treat it for what it is- a new and humbling experience.

Now, with every mountaintop experience there is typically a valley that follows. Whether it is a physical or metaphorical one, there is always a valley that awaits travelers on the other side of a climb. In our situation, our valley was returning to our homes in Miami. To be specific, most of us were heading back to Overtown.

Returning home meant we had to face reality. That reality was many times akin to the insurmountable struggles that Towners (people from Overtown) face while carrying a heart of resilience. You see, living in Overtown often felts like climbing an endless mountain, hoping that there will be a summit at the end of the climb.

I didn't grow up in Overtown but I have chosen to live there now. Overtown is my home and it is quite the complex place to live. As a result, I found myself starting to hurt alongside my community. I have started to sense the difficulty that my students, their parents, and my neighbors feel who have lived in Overtown for years. I am also learning unique ways of celebration, coping, and expressing joy. What I found in all of this is that seeking and finding God was a lot different when the valley you live in is a tough place to search...

CHAPTER 12A

Hidden Figures

I had an incredibly tender moment with one of my students yesterday. Well, technically it wasn't yesterday but it feels like it was. The memory feels incredibly fresh in my mind. Maybe it's because it's one of those memories that have shaped my life indelibly.

We were sitting in a Wendy's parking lot. We were grabbing a bite to eat. I presume we were eating something from the value menu or possibly something akin to the latest craze of "4 for 4." (That's the meal where you get four items for 4 dollars, if you didn't know). I know it was bad for our health but it was affordable and let's face it. It was comfort food for the student I was mentoring and for myself.

It wasn't the food though that was filling us up but it was rather the conversation and the presence of God. We had just dealt with a medical emergency and this mentee of mine was facing a personal tragedy of sorts. The time that we were sitting in the parking lot was a time to processes the events that just had happened. As he sat there, his whole demeanor spoke of the inner conflict he was facing. I was doing my best to be a listening ear and possibly a sounding board of sorts. He then spoke words that reduced me to rubble.

His words brought my heart and my tears low to the ground. The words echoed in my soul. They were simple but wildly painful. He sat there in a daze and with eyes filled with searching. He said, "Where is my father? I wish my father was here right now."

I knew those words very well but to see and hear them from someone else was almost too much for me to bear. My reaction time in producing tears was in nanoseconds. My empathy and sympathy reached beyond words because I understood what his soul was saying beyond the words he produced. I heard him and the millions of other souls in similar predicaments both in the US and around the world.

Although I did my best to comfort him in that moment, I also didn't try to soften or cheapen the moment that he was facing. Yes, I wanted him to feel better about what he was going through. However, I didn't want to neglect the pain that comes with fatherlessness. After all, there are just somethings that are harder without your father present. And there are some moments where you want him to be there more than others. After all, it is not something you can quantify by scientific exploration or synthesis, but there are moments in a fatherless person's life where you realize the power of what you are missing and who you are missing. For me it was that moment on that bridge. And for my student, it was that moment in the Wendy's parking lot.

That moment provoked me to once again ask and find an answer to our shared question- Where's My Father? My answer to this question is how this book came about. In this book I focused on the Heavenly Father and how I have found Him in expected and unexpected persons, places, and things.

However, there is something to be said about finding my biological father in and on this earth. Now, within this lies a difficult and concrete truth. My biological father is dead. I cannot change that. Also, I cannot change his absence in our lived and shared history. He wasn't present in my life, except for a handful of moments. Nevertheless, I have found him in a peculiar way. I have found him through hidden figures. These are men who are proxy fathers. These are men who have stepped in as father figures when my dad could not. God in his grace has provided these men at various points in my life.

In fact, my Heavenly Father has gifted me with plenty of father figures. When you see me you don't see them right away, but if you look closely you will see the impression that these hidden figures have made in my life. Each of these men in unique ways taught me lessons of life, given me pieces of wisdom, or shown me practical things I needed for everyday living.

One example is a man named Brother Tony. He was one of the elders at the church I grew up in. He and his wife, Sister Michelle, were also our youth group leaders. During the week he was a school bus driver in the Broward County School system. On the weekends, and sometimes on weekdays, he was the church van driver.

This man was a gift from God to me. Gratitude compels me to give him a shout out:

> *Brother Tony!!! Thank so much for teaching me the ways of service. You were one of the first men in my life to give me an example of what it means to be a hard worker. To work when no one is watching. To be consistent.*
>
> *Thanks for always picking up me on the church van, taking me to youth group and other youth events, and for speaking truth in my life. It was there on the church van, that you appointed*

me bus assistant. You and I would do the whole route together. Now that I write this, I realize that you were intentional to me in this regard. You were purposefully giving me responsibility and character building moments.

You would pick me up first and drop me off last. And along the way you would teach me how to serve others. Whether it was me opening the door for other youth on the church bus or cleaning when no one was watching.

During that time we chatted about God, life principles, and listened to Moody radio. Those were invaluable moments to me. You just don't know the most incredible effect that you have had on my life. I thank God for you. I don't know if I ever got to really say "thank you" to you and Sister Michelle, but thanks a ton! What a power couple you both were to us as youth.

... Brother Tony wasn't the only one. God provided an army of men to play the role of a father in my life. Edward Clarke, Justin Scott, Charles Freeman, Tony Hamilton, Blair Bailey, John Tiersma Watson, Mike Harding, Paul Neil, Drew Reyn, John Ferguson, Larry Tidwell, Karl Francis, Mark Douglas, and Oscar Siflinger are just a few men that I could name that played that unique role in my life in some way or another.

When I look at my life I have to be grateful for such men who have been faithful to God and faithful to me. Whether they did it knowingly or unknowingly they answered an ancient biblical mandate that has often gone unnoticed in our day and age. The scriptures have said, "Learn to do good; seek justice, correct oppression; bring justice to the fatherless, plead the widow's cause." Taking up the fatherless cause is what these men have done. And oddly enough, what they have done, leads me closer to the conclusion of this book. After this, there is only one chapter left. At that point we will pause this dialogue between our souls.

I'm not going to lie, I was a bit stressed out once I started writing the final chapters. Once I had gotten to this point in my writing, I developed the worst type of writer's block. After weeks of smooth continuous thoughts, I suddenly was gripped with the worst anxiety. I became overwhelmed and consumed with the idea of how I should conclude with this book.

My flaws of pride and perfectionism started to dictate my writing. Like many authors, I wanted to end with a pleasant resolution for my audience. I wanted to please you, myself, and God in one fell swoop. However, I couldn't come up with anything - nor should I. In that moment of temporary paralysis I faced a great temptation. It was the temptation for me to end this book with a neat little bow or with a cherry on the top. I was trying my hardest to think of some fantastic story to captivate you with. Something to "wow" you with. I couldn't come up with anything because I didn't have to. My life is similar to yours in this way- it is complex and yet simple. And like you, I am pretty sure you couldn't tell your whole life story in one sitting or in one setting.

There are many more things I want to say about seeking and finding God, but I am sure there will be another time for that. Or maybe another book. (Hint, hint). Instead, I want to end in this way. I want to leave you with a challenge. I am doing this because this is my nature. If you know me at all, you know that I never want myself, or my friends, to ever stay completely comfortable. So, I always ask questions to challenge them and myself.

Here's the first challenge:

Take up the cause of the fatherless. There are many young men and women who are asking the same question for which this book is entitled. The phrase "where is my father" is cried out more often than we think but it seldom heard by the people who can help answer that question or be a solution of sorts.

From where I live and where I work I see a plethora of young people who are fatherless, and many of their fathers are locked away. Some of their fathers are already dead. Some of their fathers are alive, but are absent, missing, distant, or disconnected. I also see many who are present and these men are incredible. They are the unsung heroes who father under the most strenuous of circumstances.

My challenge for you is this. Will take up the cause for the fatherless? Will you take time to look around you? Is there some child going unnoticed? Is there some son or daughter that needs an extra hand? A son or daughter who you know you could take care of? Mentor? Spend some time with? Listen to? Give advice? Be responsible for?

If they are your biological son or daughter, I ask you this. What's your excuse? Why don't you take care of your child? Why not give the best that you can give? And even if he or she is not your biological child and even if the child doesn't look like you in skin tone, hair color, dress, or demeanor, what stops you from being an answer to a simple prayer?

CHAPTER 12B

Overtown and Repentance

When I was younger I think I had a very simplistic, liberating, and pure understanding of God. Back then it seemed easy to seek and find God because my faith was matched up with my chronological age. My faith was childlike and uninhibited. This made sense because I was literally a child. When God presented Himself to me at that age, I accepted Him for who He was and as I was. There were no pretenses and second-guessing in my interactions with Him. Learning about Him and His nature was a joy, not a chore. Loving Him was effortless and desirable, not a task. I just simply presented myself to Him in trust.

To my dismay, something happened along the way. Something marred my simplistic faith. Instead of seeing God in everything and everywhere, God was narrowed to a box called the church building and its lock was religion. And the key ... well... that's what I am searching for right now, but I am guessing it has something to do with Jesus. I went from trusting God intuitively, and creatively, to becoming a mathematician in my faith. I slowly became a person who was inwardly formulaic or method-based in my approach to seeking and finding God. I guess there is nothing terribly wrong that, unless you completely displace questioning, mystery, the illogical, and tragic out of the equation.

Unbeknownst to me and my awoken consciousness, I became a slave to the laws found and connected to church buildings. I found myself in the frustration that most people have who love Jesus but have antipathy towards some institutions of church. The frustration I had was that some institutions of church seemed to be incompatible with the Church described in the Bible- especially in the New Testament. It was a place not for seeking and finding God but something altogether different. Something that made it hard to seek and find God.

I have been a part of many, many churches around the US and I have found this common, similar thread to be true. Many churches are more intimately connected to the building itself rather than to God, the people that come to them, and/or the community and environment that surrounds. The emphasis, whether blatant or inconspicuous, has a business focus. The end goal for many churches was the building itself. It was though the building had its own personality and that personality casted a spell and shadow upon the people. It was as if the building dictated how the people were to seek and find God.

Everywhere I went the emphasis seemed to be on growing the capacity and filling buildings with people but there was very little in substance about filling hearts and loving those that are unpolished, unchurched, and far from ever stepping into a church building. What was worse was that each building had its building codes. For persons to remain a part of the church, the participant must fulfill the laws and diatribes connected to the building. Or that person became ostracized from the club. The kicker though is this. God doesn't live in buildings. He lives and dwells in hearts. And those hearts are everywhere. Those hearts are also in places like Overtown.

Technically speaking, I live in an unincorporated part of Overtown. I literally live on the line where Overtown starts and ends. And where Spring Gardens starts and ends. It depends on who you ask of what my area is called, but what is definitely clear is that my job is in Overtown, my heart is in and for Overtown, and I can literally walk to most of my students homes in a minute or so.

What is also clear is that church became complicated for me once I moved into the area. Seeking God became dreadful and tiresome. And finding Him became scarce. And the worse thing was this. I started to become a little bit like the people I despised. I start to have a heart of a hypocrite. I started to become purpose-driven but not for God's purposes. I was searching and finding God for my personal gain and not for Christ-like reasons. I became a scared, timid church goer looking for self-help. I was seldom a person whose actions followed his words- at least not truly and deeply. I followed Jesus up until I reached my maximum in discomfort. At that point I had to find God in another place.

I had to start finding God in the unexpected places, in between places, and in the hearts of fearless believers. God and His presence is found in the unmentioned things, the behind the scenes, the mundane, and the unspoken. Now don't get me wrong, I still believe I can seek and find God in the local church. And still have hope in local expressions of church, but I have to admit that I find Him easier on the outside of the four walls. I find that God is doing more outside the church building than within it.

My current experience of life has me asking hard questions for myself and for others. What is that we believe about God? How do we seek and find Him in our current state of affairs? Does that theology have anything to do with the people who live in our communities? My community?

My experience had me asking those questions deliberately of Overtown. I especially have asked them as it concerns my students. My students are desperate to know God in his truest form but are quick to dismiss church because of their experiences with it. I can't blame them. I am in a similar boat. Right now I am in need of a radical but profoundly simple theology. A theology that simply is Jesus and His Good News. I need a theology that resonates with my students and my community. A theology for the hood. One where Jesus doesn't look White. A theology where Jesus actually understands suffering because it's happening all around Him every day. A theology where Jesus understands Ebonics as a regular and normative way of speaking just like any other form of English. I need a theology where Jesus eats at Snappers and not at Bonefish Grill. He eats at Popeye's and not Chick-fil-A because he understands that the government and powerful men outlined the area to limit His choices.

I would love a theology that makes sense for Jesus to know the vinegary taste found in Hot Fries and Hot Sausages, and pickled eggs. A theology that understands what a food desert is. A theology where the fight for diabetes, high cholesterol, and blood pressure is a form of oppression caused from within and outside the community. I need a Jesus in me and in my community who knows how to be a mediator between rival gangs, kids playing in the streets, single moms working hard, dads being locked up, students having a safe haven, and navigating the ever growing presence of Swale (police). I need a theology that happens before, during, and after gunshots and shoot outs. A theology for stray bullets. A theology for my students getting jumped. A theology that speaks to the heart of my students who told me they think about their safety all the time. They think about it more than dreaming about their future.

I need a theology that celebrates victories that go unnoticed in places like Overtown. I need a theology that recognizes black, brown, and other minority lives at High School graduations. This is a type of theology that notices the unnoticed. This a theology that reduces you to tears when you understand what young people go through just to make it through every day. A theology that recognizes the pain here is also found elsewhere in our nation and world in varying hues. I need a theology for abuse, trauma, and pain. And I need a theology that speaks to resilience, belly laughter, and incredible innovations that take place in the presence of minimal resources. The theology for the holistically tired and the ones who have to work twice as hard to be approved. It is for the people not judged by their character but by their skin and socioeconomic status. I need a theology that re-appropriates the concept of church because my students don't want to go to these buildings because the "Hypocrites" go there and they don't understand what the preachers do with the money during offering times. They have questions that preachers are afraid or unwilling to answer.

I need a theology that recognizes gentrification as sin. It is a sin from the heart and comfort of suburban and affluent Christianity. It is a sin of omission. I need something different because I'm drowning in the apathy that surrounds me. I know Jesus is here but I don't think people really care that much. And I am not sure that I care as much as I should, if I am honest.

What I find is that I am often tired and stressed. I have lost a little luster in my relationship with Jesus and my seeking and finding of God has been much more difficult than I expected. I know my Father is with me but I think I have drifted from trusting Him like I use to because of all the pain I see around me. Not to mention, the pain and sin I haven't dealt with inside of me.

I feel like Peter. Jesus has called me to walk out on the water with Him. Unfortunately, my eyes have drifted from him. I feel like I am sinking more times than I am walking with my Father. Little did I know that God wanted something from me too. I needed a theology but God wanted my heart. God wanted more than what my words could say. Seeking and finding God has led me to this current state in life.

God is calling me back to the simple gospel. Back to the uncomplicated. Just following Jesus and doing what He does. Following my Father.

Currently, I am in a state of surrender and prayerful repentance:

> *I repent.*
>
> *I'm sorry God. My eyes are not fixed on you. My gaze is fixed on me. My interests, whether, I say it aloud or not, has been secretly to build up my own kingdom at the expense of Your Kingdom. I am selfish and exploitative.*
>
> *I have often used you Jesus as means to my glory and benefit. In your name I have made a name for myself. And that is wrong! I am sorry for branding myself upon a Eurocentric suburban perspective. One that makes me a Messiah and not you Jesus. Forgive me Lord.*
>
> *I am sorry for making the masses happy when in my heart I know you are sad with the way the world is going presently. I can't go on entertaining people and not entertain my convictions. Your convictions!!!*
>
> *I honestly love You Jesus but I still idolize me. That has to end. I put a bold stance against my idolatry of me. I am sorry that I have constantly crafted my words and my thoughts to the whim of an invisible audience. I don't know when it*

happened, but I stopped loving You and started serving Christianity. I have become a popper and a slave to religion. And I really want to be freed from it.

I am sorry for being ever so nonchalant about justice. I believe in what you say but I don't always have the actions that follow. I can fool people but I can't fool you. You have called me to a greater degree of justice in many realms.

I am sorry God for being silent when I should speak. I am sorry for relishing comfort and not addressing the discomfort of my brothers and sisters in excruciating pain. I am sorry for not saying with my words and actions a clear admonishment that black lives do matter, that immigrant lives are being exploited, and that White Supremacy is not just in the KKK- it's actually in the DNA of a lot American blood. It just doesn't register in the way we would expect.

And I don't have to explain myself in this. I know this to be true. And I know others know it too. If you are reading this- you know it. I know it because I know You died for every life, including the ones being stolen away daily.

I am sorry for being so scared to share my story openly for fear of what people think. The truth is Jesus, you are my salvation. You are my heart. You make brave daily. I live my life solely because of You. I have no shame in that.

The truth is I am person that lives in beautiful tension. Tension with my sexuality, tension with my skin color, tension with spiritual warfare, tension with economic disparity, tension with being a prophet and speaking the clear words that God is saying to and through me.

I am sorry God.

I say this not only with my words but with my actions. I will live according to my calling. I am an usher and I am bridge.

Again, I surrender. Today I declare I will do and live better. Today, I will take up my cross and follow you, my Father...

CPSIA information can be obtained
at www.ICGtesting.com
Printed in the USA
FSHW010249030120
65695FS